Rebecca Ryan was born an child in Galway, Ireland on December 18th 1999 and now lives in County Clare where she is going into her final year at school. After that she wants to do everything.

Copyright © onstream

Text and illustrations © Rebecca Ryan
Back cover and page 183 pics: Miki Barlok
Editorial assistants: Lynn Canham, Lia Curtin

ISBN: 978 1 897685 54 9

Published in Ireland 2016 by Onstream,
Currabaha, Cloghroe, County Cork, Ireland.

www.onstream.ie

Book design: Nick Sanquest

Printing: KPS, Ireland

DICTATORSHIP

My Teenage War with OCD

Words and Illustrations

REBECCA RYAN

acknowledgements

I'd like to thank Mr Kirwin, Principal, and all the staff of Kilrush Community School for their incredible help and support.

Thank you to Dr Joe Power for giving me the push I needed to get this book off the ground.

Thank you to my amazing friends in Kilrush. Thank you to my parents, for their endless patience and support, and to the Duffy, the Rodriguez and the Kennedy-Dennehy familes, who have been there and supported me from the start.

Special thanks to Róisín, Ciera and Dr Mairéad McGovern, and to Mick Collins and Dr Michael Harty for helping me through.

Rebecca Ryan, August, 2016

CONTENTS

I'd like to dedicate this book to my amazing friends and family for putting up with me, to my wonderful school and teachers, and to every strong person out there struggling with an illness.

Prologue

I truly don't want to die.

I don't want it to be like in the movies, where children and parents alike are lured into a day of fun and happiness just before a disaster strikes. Perhaps it might be Christmas, a birthday or just a particularly good day. We get lured into a false sense of security and happiness so easily, little knowing about the shark in the water. A smarter person knows to be on their guard.

I don't want the false sense of security. I'd rather just have the storm without the calm. I don't want to be lured into happiness and then wake up in the middle of the night with my room burning, curtains flailing, parents screaming because they can't get out.

I don't want them to die in a fire.

I don't want them to go to hell.

I don't want to have to go to the police station to give my account of what happened while a bossy lady comes in and tells me both my parents are dead. I don't want to smell the dirty breath coming out from between her gapped teeth and chapped lips.

I don't want to throw myself on the ground and scream like I've been shot.

✦

Anxiety.

That's what it is.

If you can predict what your next step is in a sequence of actions, it gives a certain balance to your life. It makes you feel safe. Well, at least for me, anyway. I am not a person who is fond of changes in schedule. It throws the whole world out of kilter, and I panic. Certainty is a necessity, and predictability is compulsory.

And compulsions are mandatory.

For me, that's the way it has always been. If I am not sure of something, I will worry about it endlessly until either I get answers, or the problem is resolved. It's like my mind won't stop working overtime, and I can't stop it. I've always been a worrier, and that is not unusual. Many people are worriers, but when it gets out of hand, it can lead to problems.

My parents say that I should just stop worrying or my life will go by without having any fun. I disagree. I have to worry. It's a necessity. I'm not saying I like it, but worrying is essential for me. I hate it, yet need it.

I used to think that it was a good thing, being worried all the time. It didn't feel good, but it was my way of making sure everything was okay. When I was younger, if there was any change in routine, I would freak out, because I couldn't predict what was going to happen next. I thought that relying on the catastrophizing voice in my head made me careful, apprehensive, safer than most. I didn't think it could do me or my family any harm, but it turns out that trying to be certain all the time does more harm than good.

Soon I was trying to take control of everything, trying to be certain of everything, just to satisfy the little voice inside my head telling me the worst was going to happen.

My name is Rebecca Ryan and I am a kid with OCD, or Obsessive Compulsive Disorder. It's a condition based on severe anxiety. It's absolutely horrible to live with, and I'm still living with it, even though, technically, it's gone after absolutely AGES of it dictating my life. If you picked up this book, chances are you either have OCD, and want to know more about it, or you are just curious.

Why am I writing this book? I'm writing it to tell other people my story. I feel there is something positive I can pass on, having spent time in OCD hell. I want to contribute to the growing knowledge of OCD and help other people know what it's like.

Whatever reason you may have for picking up this book, if you continue to read it, you'll find out more about my own experience of OCD, and how I beat it in a year.

Chapter One
The Pest Explained

The sky is beautiful, or so my Mom says. I can't look at the sky. It's blue.

I don't like blue. It's a colour that reminds me of sadness. I acquired my aversion from the statement, "You're looking a little blue, aren't you?" It means sad. Whenever I see, hear or even read the word 'blue', it makes me so anxious I want to scream and run away. I feel that if I accidentally breathe in while looking at the colour, I'll acquire some of that sadness, and I can't deal with that.

I'm standing in a car park outside a local supermarket on a warm August day. Many people are either at the beach, or here, getting barbecue supplies for a house party, but all we're getting is stuff to keep us supplied at home.

When I step onto the footpath, my mind starts up, as it always does.

"Don't step on the cracks. You will die."

There it is. One thought of many.

There's no point trying to block it. The thoughts have struck again, and I must obey.

I raise myself on to the tips of my toes (not quite *en pointe*, but close enough) and begin picking my way to the supermarket entrance. I can feel my Mom's gaze burning my back. I can't help it. It's not my fault the bricks on the footpath are so small. I try to swing my arms and look carefree, so it seems that everything but my two feet are acting normally. It works up until the point where I bump into an older lady, have to apologise, and then jump the last few feet into the entrance. It's easier than continuing to tiptoe.

I also nearly crash into a couple of kids coming out of the store. Needless to say, I look like an idiot to them. But I don't care. I never cared what other kids think. I got the ritual done and that was all that mattered.

My Mom follows me in and grabs a basket, and we begin our shopping.

Shopping is boring for any kid, but I would love to be bored at this moment in time. Or maybe this whole thing has happened to me as a result of boredom.

Only now do I realise how many products have blue wrappers. Blue crisps, blue magazines, blue sandwich wrappers sitting on a shelf. Blue is not good. If there is blue around me, I have to tap my nose and 'blow away' the sadness, or the general negative effects of the trigger. Sometimes I can't get it exactly right, and have to do it again. That can take a lot of time, but I just have to go with it. But 'going with it' can take ages, and that is not ideal in a supermarket.

I tap my nose and continue shopping as if nothing has happened. Mom rolls the cart onto the Deli section, not too far from the entrance. She wants to get chicken for dinner, and I follow. It's easier to walk in this place, because the tiles are HUGE, and my crack-avoidance almost looks normal. I keep my ears cocked for people's conversations, wary that they might be saying something that may trigger anxiety. I'm at the counter now. My eyes scan the prices.

Damn.

There's both a 4 and an 8 in the price.

I tap my nose to blow away the fear.

I am terrified of the number 4, and any multiples of it, so, as with blue, I have to blow it away if I get as much as a whiff of it around.

My obsession with 4 stems from the fact that the number is associated with death in China, and, ridiculous as it sounds, I get scared due to my general fear of death. I do everything I can to avoid it.

This time, I didn't get the ritual right, and now my fear has escalated. You see, I can't blow the bad luck away near my parents, because I feel that I will pass it on to them. I have to point my non-tapping fingers away from my family, so the bad luck doesn't spray on them. It's a very complicated process. You wouldn't believe the amount of intricate rules that compulsions have.

I navigate around the aisles with Mom and see two people I know from school at the other end of the shop. I try to walk normally, but this causes me to step on a crack. I start panicking and doing a tapping compulsion to neutralise the fear. I can only hope the people in my class didn't see me. Doing something unusual sets you apart, and I sure as heck wouldn't want to be known as a freak.

After our shopping, we load our groceries into the car and I have to do more compulsions. I suddenly begin to worry that somebody I know might have seen me doing them. "I think people over there saw. I think they did. Damn it, what if they did?"

I may look crazy to them, I know, but I'm not. Being aware of your lunatic mannerisms and not being able to stop them is frustrating to say the least, terrifying at the most, but I'm not insane.

Living every day in absolute terror takes a toll on you, and in my case, that toll has been taken on my life in general. Not being able to go anywhere, do anything and speak to people was very hard. It was not nice to have to hole up on the couch or in your room, using a few select 'safe' items that didn't hold many triggers. I wasn't a recluse: I was tightly restricted.

I sure am glad I wrote that in the past tense.

OCD stands for Obsessive Compulsive Disorder. It's a mental disorder that is marked by intrusive thoughts and compulsive or repetitive behaviours. The mind designs 'rituals' to counteract the thoughts. A milder form of this condition could be called Obsessive Compulsive Tendency, but this is a sub-clinical condition and does not require diagnosis. It is only when a person's life is being put on hold for rituals that OCD can be diagnosed.

What are intrusive thoughts? They are simply normal thoughts that every person experiences. They become 'intrusive' when they make people feel scared, anxious, guilty, terrified and so on. Sometimes people get urges to do something they don't want to do. It's like their brain is poking at them, trying to get them to do dangerous things. For example, someone could be in a car and get the urge to open the door while driving at high speed. They could get so scared at having such a thought, that they'd seat themselves far away from the door and fold their arms to avoid 'temptation.'

Have you ever stood over a cooker, making dinner, and suddenly you get a flashing image in your mind: an image of the pan catching fire, the fire spreading, you engulfed in flames? You flick it out of your mind, knowing that, in all probability, it won't happen. That's an intrusive thought.

Despite their sometimes negative effects, I believe them to be critical for human survival. If we couldn't predict worst case scenarios, even at the lowest probability, we'd probably get into all sorts of trouble. The problem with OCD is, it lets these thoughts take over. We overvalue them. We can recognize the thought as irrational, but we still half-believe it. You can have many less stressful intrusive thoughts throughout the day and not even notice them. A mental illness like OCD can lead us to falling into this kind of trap.

Intrusive thoughts are an essential component of OCD. An intrusive thought could be called an 'obsession'. From my experience, an obsession is a thought that comes into a person's head that causes them discomfort or anxiety. Many of these obsessions circle around the fear of the unknown. An example of this would be "If I don't do this, something bad will happen," or "if I think about a crime scene three times, I will not lose control and hurt somebody." These thoughts repeat over and over again, and are very difficult to get rid of. Afflicted people then perform a 'compulsion', which is a repeated action or ritual to keep the obsession at bay. From this, they experience relief. Next, the person feels they must do something to counteract this bad feeling they get from the obsession. The person may perform a ritual or a behaviour over and over again until the feeling is gone. That creates the illusion of significance attached to the behaviour. The person believes that, by performing a certain compulsion, the thoughts will go away.

And when the thought comes back, what does the person do? Go on, I dare you. Guess!

Well, if you were a ninja and had one really good sword to kill an enemy with, would you use it the next time?

Of course.

It worked the first time, didn't it?

The ninja with his sword is the compulsion. The hero. The saviour. He'll rid you of those bad thoughts, only asking for a bit of attention in return. Not a bad deal. Who would guess he would take advantage and demand more and more, feeding on fear like a vampire and growing stronger and stronger.

The obsessions and compulsions begin taking up more time. You begin to feel as if you have no control. Your mind is going round in circles and you feel crazy. You feel as if you are being split in two. Half of you believes this mischievous saviour, while another half knows it's not logical and must stop at once. Days and nights are spent doing the compulsions to banish the thought. That thought that horrifies you, makes you want to cry. You can't seem to get over it, no matter how much people tell you that you have to. You have to keep doing the compulsions, washing your hands, banging the door, touching your ear, anything.

And if, over time, these obsessions keep coming back and getting stronger, and, if the person's life gets severely disrupted by this process, that's OCD.

Sufferers doubt their self-control, wondering whether they are morphing into a serial killer before their own eyes. Their filters aren't working. The mind has taken hold of the thought and twisted it, blowing it up out of proportion. But, in fact, an OCD sufferer would naver make a good serial killer We're probably the safest people to be with, in fact. We are just bombarded by ordinary, everyday thoughts that our minds have turned into worries. Those worries, if given enough attention, turn into the Os of OCD: Obsessions.

Obsessions haunt the person with OCD. People regularly use the term 'obsessed' in a good way to describe something they're really interested in. But OCD obsession is destructive.

I might have an obsession with a model bomber plane, but I enjoy it. People with the unwanted type of obsession are in constant fear of whether they might lose control and stab someone, as a result of just one thought. OCD can make you obsessively worry over just about anything, and lead to wildly irrational behaviour. That's not fun, to say the least.

The person with OCD stops and wonders why they had an intrusive thought. Anybody else would shake it off, but this person goes deeper. They begin to question whether that thought had any power. One thing I had with my obsessions was the idea that the future could be altered just by having a thought. I felt if I got a thought that my mom will die in a fire, then it could happen. That was my mindset. With OCD, you logically know there is no possible way for that to happen, but the fear takes hold of your sense of logic and overrides it. Anxiety asserts itself by overriding human common sense. There is a point where the evolutionary method of anxiety as a tool of survival starts to backfire. That is when, in response to the thoughts, OCD afflicted people experience anxiety and feel they need to do something, a compulsion or a ritual, to counteract it.

Maybe a certain action will help, they think. Anything that feels like it would negate the 'bad luck'. How about checking the stove to make sure a fire won't break out? That seems like it would help.

The person checks the oven. No fire. It's definitely off. There is no chance of it turning on by itself, is there? Nope, definitely not.

There we are. The mind is at rest. The person has stopped their mom from dying in a fire by making sure the stove is off. It seemed like the right thing to do. But what about the fireplace? That could be dangerous. The person checks the fireplace. That seems safe too. The mind is at ease. The worry is gone. Life is balanced again.

The trouble is that this thought has now had too much attention. Anybody else would have dismissed it. This is how OCD develops. If the person was vulnerable to the thought the first time, I wonder what would happen if it were to come back?

And then it does.

At this, the person will check again. Their mind keeps telling them that their mom will die in a fire, and, even though they know it's illogical, they are at a loss to know what else to do to keep her safe. Soon they are fixated on the danger. The habit begins to form. The checking becomes compulsory, meaning they must do it, or endure the anxiety. It's now the C of OCD, a Compulsion. If they don't do it, their mom will die in a fire. You wouldn't risk someone's life like that, would you?

It becomes a vicious cycle. The person's life starts getting disrupted, as they begin focusing on the compulsion rather than daily activities. Trust builds between the person and the compulsion, and a sort of mental crutch is formed. The compulsion soon has priority over everything else. Soon, the presence of the lifesaving compulsion turns into a threat of, "If you don't do that, your mom dies."

Now, they also start to beat themselves up for being weak, and giving in, even when they know it's not rational. They aren't delusional, you know. They just can't put logic over fear. With fear, comes the flight-or-fight reaction. The initial reaction of anyone when confronted with fear is to flee. You can then learn how to fight.

Have you ever received chain mail? I saw some online, and I realised that it was almost exactly the same as the obsessional component of OCD, designed to lure you in. Have you ever opened an email, only to read, "If you don't post this to 10 people in your friend's list, your mother will be killed in 365 days"?

Does that seem rational, or even possible to you?

And yet, thousands of people passing them on every day. I bet most, if not all, of those people have a grasp on logic. You may judge them as being stupid, but they're not. Many will attach significance to something that is written and well explained. It's a form of superstition. Why are people passing on these messages? Because they aren't sure whether or not that event is going to happen. It's probably not going to happen, but, they figure, who knows? The repetitive posting of the comment works like the compulsion in OCD. The action has been completed. No need to worry anymore.

OCD is mental chain mail. Only, it doesn't get passed on to someone else. It's stuck inside your head all the time and it hurts. However, you can learn to beat it. It can get easier. I've certainly found it easier to ignore chain mail ever since I got rid of my OCD. According to my social media, I should be dead by now.

Imagine those sort of threats going through your head every minute of every day and night. It's extreme dictatorship.

That was the O and C of OCD. The last part of OCD is probably the most important part: Disorder. The Disorder component of OCD is important because there has been a lot confusion between definitions of compulsive behaviour and OCD.

Have you ever heard the cliché that somebody with OCD needs to have everything perfect? Something I can't stress enough is that it is not always the case! If more people understood the D in OCD, a lot of the confusion between compulsive behaviour and OCD would be cleared up. It would be lovely if everyone knew about OCD like they know about cancer or diabetes. I'm not saying it's always as severe as those awful diseases, but people do need to wake up to how destructive it can be. Yet so few understand it. Some teachers or doctors do, because they're supposed to know stuff like that. Kids don't know about it unless it's happened to them or to someone they love. Yet, everybody knows about asthma, diabetes or the flu. When it comes to something mental, people are, like, "What the hell?"

The thing is, we OCD people are weird. We have to line pencils up in class before we can even begin to listen to the teacher. We are the ones who don't volunteer an answer to a simple question in the schoolroom. All the other hands are up, and time seems to stand still while the teacher waits for a response. Fact is, we never heard the question to begin with.

The ones with 'selective' OCD take pride in their clothes looking their best, or colour-coding their nail varnish. They're the ones with the tidy lockers or sanitiser in their back pockets. It's a cute and quirky variation on OCD, and DEFINITELY something to tweet about with a cute little hashtag.

I have OCD, yet I don't need to have everything perfect. I'm not scared of germs. I couldn't care less, to be quite honest, and I'm not the only person to feel this way. Fear of germs and having everything perfect are variations of symptoms of OCD, but it isn't that black and white. In fact, it's grey, with little white streaks running carelessly through it, only to be spattered with black dots. It's unpredictable, like my mom watching a football match. It's a whirlwind of thoughts rolled up so it looks like a tunnel, the biggest scariest fears are the closest, and the everyday thoughts are shoved way down to the end, diminishing in size and importance. The thought's proximity represents its intensity. And its control.

People with OCD are stuck in this tunnel. They need to get through it to the freedom, but they just can't seem to get away from the thoughts and fears that keep pulling them back. It's not an addiction, it's a reliance which soon becomes a dependency. Ultimately, it's a threat.

The OCD sufferer is stumbling around in the darkest part of the tunnel. They can see the light at the end, but they aren't sure whether it's freedom, or an oncoming train. There are bound to extra-springy restrictive cables, stuck to the wall, which yank them back whenever they try to rush forward. They know that they would be able to break free of the cables if they could pull hard enough. But pulling hurts and they are scared of the rebound. If they try harder, the cable's intensity might yank them back more painfully. Surely it would be easier to just stay where you are and comply, than to go through all that pain and still maybe not make it through?

That's where they are wrong. They need to keep pulling, no matter how painful it is, and soon they will break free, and run to the freedom they deserve.

But it's not easy, and it's not pretty.

OCD is not a quirk. It's a pest, a parasite. It's the one insect that you can't find the right bug spray for.

I wrote this book to contribute to the firewall against misinterpretation. I just want to help. I also want to talk to other kids with OCD and tell them that they'll be fine. Nothing is going to happen. Nothing at all, believe it or not. Of course, you already know that, don't you? Yet, you just can't be certain. None of us can. The only solution is to beat it, and that's coming from a kid with it. I don't know you, or your OCD type, but if you have it, there is no excuse not to beat it. You may be scared, but that's just like going on your first rollercoaster ride. You don't know what to expect and it's terrifying.

Here's a secret: a rollercoaster is worse.

Chapter Two
It Emerges

I remember being at the playground in our local town when I was four. It was my usual haunt with Mom, after we did the grocery shopping.

On this particular day, I got stuck on the climbing bars. There was a set of them which led to the top of the slide, way up high. You could either slide down from there, or proceed to the monkey bars. I wanted to go on the slide, but all the other kids were in front of me.

I decided to wait until the coast was clear, so no other children could kick me in the back if they went down the slide too quickly after me. When they'd moved on, I began my ascent up the four-foot climbing bars. I was sure I could make it to the top. Halfway, I got stuck.

I stayed there for a while, debating on how to get up, or back down. Then I heard my Mom call me from the car, where she sat while I played. "What are you doing? Are you going up or coming down?"

"I don't know."

"Go on, you can do it."

So I tried to climb up, but then I saw the top. My four-year-old body froze. It was too good to be true that I could get up there. I could fall through the bars. And I was getting weird urges.

Urges to let go and lean back. To make myself fall off the bars.

I began to feel a need to make myself risk falling off, to let go for at least one second and see how long I could go without teetering over. I needed to desperately. The urge to do so kept building up until I felt like screaming so, all at once, I let my hands loosen their grip. I began to lean backwards. In a fright, I grabbed on again. But I had to keep pushing it. I must keep loosening my grip on the bars. It felt right.

My Mom, watching this, ran over and grabbed me.

"What are you doing?"

She suggested I play on the swings instead, so I ran over and grabbed the low one.

This time I had a method.

I jumped up on the lower of the two swings and began to rock. I made sure I was swinging steadily, not dangerously, but so that it would certainly hurt if I were to fall off. The urges were picking at me, screaming for me to let go. But just letting go wouldn't be enough. I had to be going higher and faster. I had to feel scared for the task to be successful.

So, in rapid mid-swing, I loosened my grip and flung myself forward. I couldn't begin to save myself until I was scared enough. I had to count the seconds I could last on the flailing swing without falling. But, every time I got scared a little more, the bar would have to be raised. My mind kept telling me I could do better, that I could get more scared than that. As a result, I had to keep swinging without holding on until I was at such a risk of flying off that I had to grab the handles or get a face full of playground dirt.

At the last possible moment, I grabbed hold again, breathing heavily. I screamed a little. I genuinely thought I was going to go flying through the air. I could visualise it happening, and it was scary.

But I had completed the task, and everything was okay again.

Fast forward to now, and that initial impulse had turned into something bigger than I had thought. I never thought I would have to go to a doctor for anything other than a check-up. Well, except for the Great Stomach Virus of 2008. That was scary too.

But things happen that we don't anticipate, and we just have to deal with them. Some take longer than others to sort out. I'm not wise. I'm just a kid. But this is my educated guesswork and I think it's pretty accurate.

I'm a worrier. A lot of people are. It's not unusual. But, if it gets out of hand, a little bully may set up shop in your head, and that can be seriously annoying. However, before this catastrophizing house of cards can be built, a foundation has to be laid down. That foundation is anxiety.

Anxiety is a common feeling, but it can multiply without being noticed. That's one of the reasons, I believe, that it is so easy for a person to suffer from an anxiety disorder. Nobody knows it's sneaked up on them until it's right in their face.

I wasn't always anxious, though. I was very sassy when I was younger. I used to run up and down the hall in our old house singing 'Satisfaction' by The Rolling Stones, and liked to draw on old bits of paper Dad brought home from work. My favourite thing, though, was to spend hours and hours writing and illustrating stories. I'd invent a new character every day and build a whole world around them. I spent a lot of my childhood searching online for publishers and organisations. I'd always make plans to send stuff off to them, but I never did.

I'm a really hyper kid, and was like that even in the periods where OCD didn't really bother me as much. Because of this, my Mom had me going to karate, dancing and piano classes all week to keep me occupied.

Alongside this healthy author ambition, I started to develop a lot of unhealthy anxiety. Except, when you're a kid, you don't know it's anxiety, it's just a feeling that colours your thoughts and actions.You go along with it. You aren't conscious of whether it's logical or not. And in most cases, it isn't.

I used to feel like I needed to know that I would be going to bed at a certain time, no extensions or early sleeping. I couldn't just take a nap on the couch. Sleeping was for bedtime. That was the routine.

I felt like I needed to know when to be told to stop reading before going to sleep. I couldn't just put myself to sleep. It needed to be official.

When I was small, if my parents told me they were going out on the following Saturday, I would be in a panic for the week leading up to it. And yes, I would have to be told in advance. Heck, in January, I would start to worry about my parents going to the next Christmas dinner dance! My tummy would churn, I would feel sick, and little knots of fear would scrape my insides. It would consume my thoughts all through the school day and get worse when it was home time. That's on the good days. I'd look at their night out as being doomsday. I would walk out of the classroom on the Friday afternoon before 'armageddon' and think, "I wonder what will happen in the space of time between now and the next time I see this room. How will the Night Out have gone?"

I would try and look to the Rebecca in the future, who already experienced the night out, and ask her how it went.

I was scared for myself. I was scared because the routine was changing. Routine was my world. I was scared for my parent's safety. I was going to be without my parents, my lovely parents, and I couldn't keep an eye on them. I couldn't make sure that they were okay. Anything could happen to them out there, and I wouldn't be able to save them.

Around those times, my compulsions would intensify.

I didn't know what to do with my time while they were out. I hated the disruption. I knew I had to get past it, but I just found it so scary that I couldn't. I would record a load of TV programmes the week before the Night Out, counting the hours it would take to watch them, enough to fill the hours up to bedtime. Then I would arrange some activities I could do, just in case, so I had plenty distractions. I had to make sure my parents followed a very strict timetable, so that I could absolutely rely on their departure and arrival times.

✦

I've had compulsions since I was small. They were subtle at first, and hard to distinguish from normal kid behaviour. For example, when I started primary school I didn't really like it on the first day. That's normal. But on the second day, I ran screaming out of the school after my Mom shouting, "Mommy! Don't leave me here! I'll die if you leave me!"

From then on, I knew my favourite class would be Drama.

It was like that for the first few days, and the teacher even had to break out the crow puppet to cheer me up (I was actually mystified about how it made its noise, but I found out that you just squeeze its beak).

I started to get really, really worried about school every morning. I got so scared that I developed little 'habits' (which is what I call my compulsions) that I had to do each morning before school. I had to make my Mom wait in the hall while I dug through my toys in the playroom to find the one 'special' toy.

Some days it could be a tiny piano for my dolls, or a little plastic man with a blue jacket. It didn't matter. If I found it special, I had to give it to my mom, and inexplicably make her promise to show it to her work colleagues. I remember I would start to panic if she didn't agree. I wouldn't have a good day at school. I don't know how I came to the conclusion that picking a special toy would impact my day at school, but it stuck. That was my first of many mental crutches.

But soon, I began to have some fun at school. Well, except for the time I threw up all over the floor and the other kids couldn't get to their lunch boxes. They weren't impressed.

I met two girls in the class below me and we soon became best friends. We would go around in a threesome in the schoolyard, pretending to be puppies. We were all in love with dogs.

When I was six, I started to get serious about writing. I kept little copybooks filled with ideas and drawings and characters that I could use for a book. I used to get really excited about going home so I could work on the computer all night. I also started Irish dancing, Hip-Hop and Karate. I didn't really like Irish dancing because you weren't allowed to move your hands. I just wanted to flail about. Karate was fun. Sometimes I would get frustrated that I couldn't do the moves correctly, but it was okay because Mom gave me a little pep-talk before going into class. "Do your moves like you're attacking Bin Laden, Rebecca," she would say. Mom had me up-to-date on politics and terrorists.

But, I can remember some mini-compulsions already creeping their way to the surface.

The first one was a feeling of unevenness. I remember having to make this weird grunting noise in the back of my throat all the time to combat it. It would be me playing with a hoop in the yard, making a weird noise. I don't know where it came from, or what happened to it, but I grew out of it eventually. It may have just been a silly little-kid thing, but Mom used to give out to me for it. It annoyed her immensely. I remember why I had to do it too. It made everything feel balanced. If I resisted doing it, nothing felt right. It was like telling me not to scratch that powerful itch on the back of my head. Resistance was irritating and it made me scared. It was easier to just go along with it.

The same feeling went with writing certain things at school. We would do lessons on prices, and we weren't supposed to write the 'c' for cent if we included the Euro symbol. I felt I had to put €2.00c instead of €2.00. That annoyed both me and the teacher.

But the thing is, some things that were insignificant to others were hugely significant to me. Everything I did was compulsive.

Every day, after dinner, I would get a 'surprise', which might be a chocolate bar or a pack of jellies. Every time I got it, I had to leave one piece of it for my mom and dad. I had to go to them and ask whether they'd like to eat it. If I thought they didn't hear me, I'd repeat the question, even if I logically knew they DID hear me.

Sometimes, I wouldn't leave them enough of my surprise and I'd get bombarded with guilty thoughts. You see, if I didn't leave them enough of my treat, my mind would start saying, "You don't care enough about them to leave them a bigger piece. You are ungrateful and don't deserve them. I'll just take them away from you. Then you'll learn." A six year-old can't figure out or rationalise that kind of mental terrorism. You can't escape it. You're too young to know how.

The bombardment went on, but much of it was unconscious. OCD dictated how I'd fall asleep at night, how I'd watch TV, whether I'd stay up until 10:01 or go to bed at 10. Everything had significance. It was awfully black and white.

I went to this cute little primary school tucked up in the countryside, where everything was routine and we all knew each other. I loved that school. I still do. Thinking about it now, I had some compulsions and obsessions during school times too, but strangely enough, I never questioned why they were there or wondered whether the other kids didn't have them. I don't think I cared, either. I just kept them to myself.

I didn't walk on cracks, and I had a special routine for walking up the school steps (I always had to finish on my right foot). I also had to touch and tap things until they felt 'right', and only then could I get on with my activities. I remember I wasn't able to play this game called 'Boxes', where you stand on an area in the schoolyard where the folds of concrete meet, and swap places with somebody. One person is left out and has to try to get into the box.

I walked in circles on my own, bouncing a basketball.

A frequent trigger for my OCD was routine change. This has been the case ever since I was small. I have always needed to have everything exactly the same, the same food at restaurants, the same shopping stores, and the same daily pattern. If there was even the slightest deviation, I would feel the anxiety creeping up on me. There would be a feeling of uneasiness and apprehension growing and growing until I was panicking inside my head, wondering what was happening.

If we went as far as another county on a day out, I'd become anxious if we weren't doing structured things like shopping (you work out the price, you pay for a product, and you get out. Simple). Driving home from Limerick in the dark with a rock CD playing in the car made me anxious. It wasn't the dark or the rock music I was scared of. I was scared because the two were combined to form a new situation. Not knowing explicitly how it would feel to be back at home until I got there, was scary.

I couldn't plan my reactions. I couldn't plan anything. I would restrict my family by freaking out over the slightest thing, such as going anywhere new. In a new place, I would feel myself growing more and more superstitious. "If that door is open, nobody I am related to on my Mother's side of the family will die. If the radio presenter doesn't say the word 'Christmas' in the next ten words, we are safe from a car crash."

I couldn't really help this when I was younger, because I had no clue what was happening. My mind was always two leaps ahead of itself, and it always wanted to go somewhere else. That would probably have been rectified if I had been busy with work, but what work can a six-year-old do? I needed something to focus on, and instead became latched on to worries.

When I was ten, things really ratcheted up. I had developed a lot of compulsions to make things feel 'right' or balanced, and they were becoming more noticeable.

I had no idea at the time where these compulsions came from, and I could just about put up with them, so I just got on with it. I remember my parents and I beginning to call them 'habits' because it was the only way to describe them. So now they were so noticeable enough to be named.

I don't think my parents understood what they were. Dad told me that he used to do small rituals as well when he was young, and that my auntie would make fun of him because of it. He had to do a specific flapping movement with his hands when touching doorknobs. I was fascinated by this. I didn't know that other people did this stuff, and that was the first time I'd actually thought about the possibility that they might. I remember the endless promises at Lent to stop my habits until Easter. I remember feeling horrible because I felt I'd let God down for not fulfilling my 'penance' (as I would inevitably fail), which made me do even more compulsions.

I had now started to wear glasses, and one of my compulsions was to look into the corner of them and swirl my head around and around. It just felt right. I know I looked like an idiot, but I couldn't help it, and it made the tempest inside my mind calmer. If I even thought about not doing the compulsion, the storm turned into a hurricane, which felt horrible.

My grandparents used to always keep a light on in their shed in the evenings and, as we lived next door to them, I could see it every night from my window. I remember I had to trace around the light using circular motions of my head, and if I got it wrong, I had to start over again. It took a good twenty minutes trying to get it precisely right, and, even if I didn't even know why I was doing it, it felt right, and I felt scared if I didn't do it.

I had to touch things in fours, do a special foot tapping sequence in fours, and occasionally say things four times. I also had to use the word 'maybe' at the end of every sentence, because I felt that if any part of the sentence was incorrect, I would be punished for lying. Recently, I was looking at the videos I made with my webcam when I was ten, and I saw myself doing a compulsion. I said the exact same sentence four times, leaning into the camera exactly the same way each time. It reminded me of how odd it used to be.

Let's just say that for ANYTHING I was scared of, whether it was the 'battery low' sign on the alarm clock or the 'low flow' light on the shower (weird, I know), I would develop rituals to stop myself from being scared. I'm not even sure why I was scared of so many things. I was scared of the TV in my room, and my compulsion for that was to say nice things to it so it wouldn't get mad at me. I wasn't crazy. I knew it was ridiculous. But I felt I had to ask the television about its day, tell it about my day, and compliment it as much as I could. If I didn't, I felt it would get angry with me and hurt me in my sleep. I had nightmares about it. The fear was utterly and totally stupid, but I felt the TV was alive. It's broken now, eight years old, and permanently on my dresser. It still freaks me out a little bit, and I'm sixteen, for God's sake.

Things went on like that all the way through my pre-adolescent existence. School was fine. I was fine. Everybody was fine. My OCD hadn't completely taken over. It was only a baby and was a heck of a lot milder. I didn't know that it would get so much worse.

Life could still be fun. I went to my friends' houses to play pretend games and connected our Nintendos. It was great. We were easily entertained and content for hours. I don't think that has changed and, even though I'm now sixteen, I still play Animal Crossing.

+

Having turned twelve, I started secondary school on August 28th, 2012 at 9am. How's that for exact information? I remember the date, because things were about to get a lot worse.

Walking into such a foreign area that was supposed to be new my place of learning was a strange experience. I was open to the idea of secondary school (my approval was irrelevant because I knew I'd have to go anyway), but I couldn't see myself getting used to it.

My cuddly little primary school was so different from this rushing, elongated place with long corridors and pushing teenagers. None of us First Years were used to it. I even found it weird to see buildings across the road from the school. I was used to seeing trees and fields. I was extremely rigid with my loyalty to my primary school. I couldn't foresee a time when I would think this new place would be ok. I missed my old school terribly. After all, you can't really play at pretending to be a dog at secondary school without getting odd looks.

I had been the only girl in my class of five at primary school. It was certainly a bit strange having other girls in my class at secondary, and a big change from school being so small that four classes would be crammed into one room. But that had been the fun of it.

Now, here was just one class to each room, yet the amount of kids per room was the same, so it wasn't too different. Going from being the oldest in the old school to being the babies of the new one was odd too. Everybody was so tall. We were at butt level with them.

Even so, I began to enjoy it. I liked all the teachers, I liked the fact that we had all these different rooms to walk to, and I liked the fact that I could get lost.

I also became a huge fan of the band Passion Pit. The annoying part? Nobody at school knew about them until I told them. Well, I'm sure some did, but whoever I asked just gave me a blank face. I listened to their music all the time and … I was obsessed.

It was during this time I made a wonderful friend called Hannah. She came up to me on the first day and asked whether I'd like to hang out. I was unsure about whether she was called Hannah or Anna, but found out eventually. I was then introduced to a whole group of people including Caitlin, Eva and Hazel during the course of the year. They were and still are my best friends, along with Sylvia from primary school.

I think my favourite First Year subjects were probably Art and English. I liked History too, but I would only concentrate on the things I was really interested in, like Ancient Rome. Ancient Rome was really cool to me. I know that their kitchens were called *culina* and their bedrooms, *cubicula*. I'd sit by myself in Art, but I wouldn't care. The people were lovely, everyone was lovely, but I was content to be by myself, which sounds really rude, but I honestly didn't mean it that way.

I absolutely resented lino-printing in Art, because it was so boring. I loved the rest of Art, though. It wasn't really a class to me at all. It was just plain fun. Our Art room is really big, and covered in student's artwork. It was just a really friendly atmosphere. I wanted to draw all day. I love drawing, always have, always will. Just give me a pencil, some paper and let me off. Actually, I'd probably need a sharpener too.

There was just this overall feeling that went with being a First Year at secondary school. It felt special and unique. I want to note that the first year of secondary school isn't just a new year at school. It has a feeling with it. Every year does. That one was brilliant.

I remember being conscious of my compulsions in First Year, but I didn't see myself as being different from anybody else. I didn't give it any thought. I was used to it, and it was almost unconscious. I had OCD tendencies, but these were still very minor. I could shake them off if I wanted to, but sometimes I still had to comply with their demands.

Sometimes I had to turn my locker dial around a couple of times and tap things in a certain way, but it didn't impede my school life too much, so it was ok. I'm not saying I went around free as a bird, but everything was fairly simple. I went with the flow.

I wasn't even aware that compulsions could be set in stone. I just did them. It was easy. I think that's where I fell into the trap. Christmas of 2012 was just one big trap. And wasn't it just perfect when I fell right in?

Chapter Three
New Ideas

The changes that took place during the Christmas to January period of 2012/13 were not subtle, to say the least. It was like my OCD suddenly exploded. Over the course of a month I went from having manageable compulsions to being the focus of a blizzard of internal mental threats, repetitive actions and self-berating for giving into these blasted things. How did this happen?

Well, I wish I knew.

I was becoming even more obsessive, and things that previously didn't bother me started to. I was straightening everything. Next thing I know, I'm scared of all medical words, and I have to avoid those too. I never used to have to do that. Now they're a trigger.

I would usually get scared and nervous around Christmas because there's no routine. Sometimes I think I am a wuss for sticking to rigid patterns all the time, but if I don't have them, it's like pulling the plug on my safety and security, and so I've always found holidays crazy. You open presents in the morning instead of getting breakfast, and you eat a different kind of dinner, and decorations that usually aren't there are put up all over the house. You stay up much later than usual and there's no set time for bed. You may be thinking, "Opening PRESENTS?! How terrible! Seriously Rebecca, cop on."

I know I have to cop on, but it makes me anxious.

Usually, on family occasions, I rely a little bit more on my compulsions to keep me safe, but in the Christmas of 2012, things went overboard just as I was also turning thirteen. I let my OCD take me over, because I trusted it. I knew what I was doing was wrong, but I was so scared, I couldn't refuse. It was like a curse had been awakened. I gradually got tied up with more and more restrictions, and found I couldn't do anything but comply with my obsessions' demands.

I put up no resistance to anything I was scared of. Everything became an obsession. January was just a slow car crash.

By February of 2013, I had many rules that I had to adhere to. Here are some of them:

1. As I said earlier, I began to avoid the number 4 as much as I could. I couldn't say it, read it, write it or hear it without anxiety, which made Maths a living hell. To relieve this, I had a compulsion of tapping my nose and 'blowing away' all the badness from the number.

2. I had developed my fear of the colour blue because to me it represented sadness. I was really scared of sadness, so, like the number 4, I avoided it at all costs, even the mention of it. I did my nose-tapping thing with this too.

3. I couldn't walk on cracks. This was a pretty normal one, because I'm pretty sure everyone does this at least once in their lives. A couple of people noticed this at school, which was not so good, and it was great fun walking in the kitchen at home, as it was tiled!

4. I had a mortal fear of any word that represented a disease, death or any other unpleasant thing. I was scared of the words cancer, death, dying, ambulance, surgery, operation, scalpel, surgeon, hospital and loads more. Sometimes the list got bigger, especially if I was worried about something in particular.

5. I had to keep everything perfectly symmetrical. I had to have everything straight. Nothing could be strewn all over a table. It had to be perfectly in line, not even slightly crooked. That might seem manageable, but I have seen the sunrise on multiple occasions, when I was up all night, straightening and checking the symmetry of everything. I would panic if stuff wasn't straight. At least my friends got something out of it – whenever I would visit, they were left with a tidy room.

6. I was scared of wood knots. You know, the little brown marks you get in wood, showing where the branches were? To me, these resembled tumours, and, since I was scared of this sort of stuff already, I had to avoid everything with knots on it. Unfortunately, the whole house was covered in them, because my parents loved wood. For a whole year, I had to close my eyes when going from room to room so I wouldn't see them. I did the nose-tapping thing for that, too.

7. Doorways. Oh man. The damn doorways. Those babies were my worst enemy. How I longed for no doorways anywhere while I struggled with this! I had to do a special tapping sequence with my feet for each panel of a door, twice if it was a set of double doors. Annoyingly, I was so used to this that I did it automatically, without even realising. Then my mind would snap back to reality, and question whether I had really, actually done it, so I had to be extra mindful to keep track of my compulsions, going, "Okay, I just did the compulsion. Tick! That's noted in my brain."

8. This one is embarrassing. I had to lift my leg higher than every object in a room, from the perspective of wherever I was in that room. That meant raising my foot and lining it up from my point of view as if it was above the whole doorframe, above the big mirror and mantel piece, everything. And sometimes my brain told me I hadn't actually lifted my leg high enough, so I had to lift it extra high. I had to do that most nights in the sitting room before I could leave it to go upstairs to bed.

9. I had to say "maybe", after everything, because I was scared if the sentence I had just spoken was incorrect, I would get punished for lying. This also applied to writing. Saying or writing "maybe" was like a get-out clause in a contract.

10. I had to count every word I wrote to make sure it didn't end up as part of a multiple of four. Preferably, it would end up in a multiple of three. This really slowed me down at school and made my writing look horrible. I put in so many extra words that my sentences were so messed up and made no sense.

11. When inserting a round plug, such as one for a laptop charger, I'd have to tap it a certain number of times without blinking. It would take me 20 minutes to get the damn charger connected. Apple devices, for example, were fine, because they were rectangular. The round ones were the problem.

12. Every thought had to be monitored. I was not allowed to think of anything medical-related or illness-related, of death, of bad numbers, of anything. I was not allowed to think about Mom and Dad. I was not allowed to picture them in my head like anybody does in a fleeting thought. I'd be penalised if I did. I was not allowed to think about routine, because I felt like it would be changed as a punishment for thinking about it. This obsession is extremely hard to explain, but it comes down to the concept that restricting a thought will encourage it even more. Monitoring had circumstance-based concrete clauses in its contract with me, and only my brain could understand how to follow it.

13. I had to pick up my schoolbooks or other items (such as pencil cases) and drop them repeatedly over and over on my desk at school. I had to pick the heaviest pile of books (or whatever I had) and raise them high above my desk and drop them suddenly. I imagine I must have annoyed the class quite a bit with this one.

14. Sometimes I would have to complete special 'challenges' my mind set for me, such as getting out of bed before the chorus began in a song I was singing in my head. If my parents went out (yes, I was still scared of that) I would sometimes have to wash my hands a certain number of times without hitting them off the sink.

These were the main compulsions I had to do, but I had more accumulating day by day. I had compulsions in the tens, maybe even hundreds.

I was so shocked at these transformations that I started keeping a diary so I could keep track of them. I didn't have a clue as to what was happening or why I had to adhere to these rules, but I was extremely angry at whatever was malfunctioning in my brain. On the ninth of February 2013, I kicked off my journal with an optimistic sentence:

9/2/13

Today is going to be a horrible day for my rituals. I already know that, and it's not yet even eleven in the morning.

Mom and Dad are mad at me for doing rituals, but I can't stop. Doing them is a small price to pay to avoid being scared all the time. I'd do virtually anything to stop that. I can't live with the fear that someone may pass away because I didn't do a ritual.

I'm constantly doubting stuff. I keep worrying that Mom or Dad has a serious illness that they are keeping from me. I constantly think, "What if?"

My habits are keeping me from enjoying First Year. I have the Principal looking at me when I do stepping rituals. He has definitely noticed. I see others staring at me, trying to be polite.

Once I get a thought in my head, it's like my brain won't let it go until I do a ritual. It's a matter of something feeling 'right'. If I step in a place that doesn't feel right, I have to do it again. And again.

If I try to resist, I get so uncomfortable. In the classroom, I can't concentrate on anything. To try to resolve this, I do a ritual and, while I'm doing it, my mind is adding ten more to the list, and then I have to do THOSE, and it gets so damn FRUSTRATING!

By the time I've finished, I have no clue what the teacher is saying and I don't even know what the class is studying.

I'm at the end of my tether and I'm cheesing everybody off, and people think I can just stop with willpower but I really flipping CAN'T!

This went on for a while. It's one thing to list all the compulsions, but to show how they impact on your life can be harder.

I'd have to hug the walls as I walked around the house just to make sure I wouldn't bump into anything. My parents were wondering what the hell was going on, especially when I spent two hours dragging my foot along the edge of the skirting board in the hall. Speaking of the hall, I began to avoid it at all costs, because it was the place where most of the wood knots were.

I began to avoid going through the front door, and either went out through the back door, or climbed out the window. The whole house became a huge obstacle course. Because I did my stepping rituals for doorways so often, they began to worsen and, as I call it, morph. With morphing, you get an idea that if you added another part onto the ritual, then it may work better. It keeps going until the ritual has completely evolved from what it was before. It's like a snake constantly shedding skins to expose new ones. Completely new, improved, but used for the same purpose. It is also just as slithery.

I told my parents, but they said I'd grow out of it. They were sure that it was just a silly fad. They were not inclined to chalk down every abnormality to some sort of illness, and I thank them for that. Even so, I wasn't convinced. It's not that I didn't trust what my parents were saying, it's just that I felt there was more going on. One night, I waited until my mom was in the bathroom and secretly recorded a TV programme on OCD from the Home & Health channel. I would need to be careful in choosing my time to watch it, as I knew my Mom would give out to me for self-diagnosing. I don't like it either, but I wanted to know more.

The show followed three people who had severe OCD. It showed all their compulsions, what effect these had and why they did them. One pulled all her hair out. One couldn't stop shutting the door. I related to everything they said. I cringed every time I saw a ritual being performed. It was like watching myself in other peoples' bodies.

One day I was watching it while Mom was upstairs. I knelt on the couch, keeping both eyes on the TV, yet peripherally scanning the stairs. But she knew what I was up to, and stormed in giving out. "Turn that off! That OCD programme! I'm not having you watch it!" I had to delete it there and then. I actually didn't mind, as I'd seen enough. Those people, doing their compulsions on TV, looked just like me doing mine. I took the possibilty of a condition like OCD just being a fad into account, but I was almost sure I had it. I didn't know how to go about making myself heard.

I decided just to go full on. I told my Mom one night what was happening, because I was completely and utterly sick to the back teeth of it. I decided not to use the label of 'OCD', as I didn't want to sound like I was self-diagnosing, so I only described what had been going on in my head, that I was imagining threats every day, and they were driving me insane. I told her I was certain it wouldn't go away on its own, and it was really affecting my school work.

It was sincerely the best conversation I'd had all year. Afterwards, we had a long discussion about how much it was affecting my life and why. Mom agreed to talk to the doctor.

The next day Dad went with her to the Medical Centre. It felt eerie that that they would be going to see a man in a white coat about their crazy daughter, even though I had initiated the visit. I just felt strongly this was something that the doctor should know about. After the consultation, they came in the car to pick me up after school, and I couldn't wait to hear exactly what had happened.

Mom told me that the doctor had started laughing at their serious faces, and that, when my parents told him about what had been going on, said that all kids display these kind of symptoms and that it can be hard to distinguish normal kid behaviour from OCD. However, he said if we were really worried, he would refer us to a therapist and a psychiatrist.

I needed to hear all this again and again. I needed to know every single detail of that appointment. Everything had significance.

I repeated the events of the appointment in my head over and over, not as a compulsion, but because I couldn't quite believe it. These things I considered normal all my life were being discussed with people I didn't know. I know I started it, but it felt surreal.

It took a little while for the referral to come through, and I was really impatient. I also couldn't help being angry, because my OCD was worsening all the time, and life was getting harder to handle as the days went by.

27/3/2013

I HATE THIS FLIPPING WAITING! I CAN'T WAIT ANY LONGER TO SEE THE OCD THERAPIST!

I CANNOT DO ANYTHING! I LEAVE THE HOUSE THROUGH THE WINDOW BECAUSE IT'S TOO HARD TO GET THROUGH THE DOOR! I CAN'T WRITE WITHOUT COUNTING MY WORDS! I DON'T WANT TO LEAVE A ROOM BECAUSE

I CAN'T!

I'M GOING CRAZY!

I watch everyone just walking around, being normal, but I can't, because I'm being bullied BY MYSELF!

I just want to meet ONE person with OCD. Just ONE!

It's like there's this gigantic wall and I'm on one side and everybody else is on the other side.

I hate it! If I lie in bed, my thoughts will RACE! They won't leave me alone. All these scary thoughts about bad things happening to my family and triggers and obsessions race around in my head, while I'm just there praying to fall asleep. I don't want to have OCD!

But it may not even BE OCD. I haven't been diagnosed.

I resent my house. I know it too well and the habits I've cultivated there are sticking.

I just don't want to get up in the morning.

I FEEL SO DESPERATE! You know how long I've had OC tendencies? SINCE I WAS 4.

Now, it's blown up! It's taking my life over!

"What if something bad happens today?"

Then I'll get thoughts like, "I am terrible to worry something bad will happen when I have such a good life and the reason something bad may happen is because I am ungrateful and doubting. It's ultimately my fault if it happens. It's my punishment for being ungrateful."

These thoughts come in a millisecond, like a lightning strike. They hit me so fast and scare the crap out of me!

Then I'm snapped back to reality and I'm so amazed that the bad thing didn't happen already because, even though I know it isn't true, it felt so REAL.

My compulsions were getting worse and worse. I had begun to fear and avoid the colour blue and the number 4, for reasons you already know. It may seem stupid to be scared of something so random, but that's how it was – I can't explain it away.

The doorways thing was getting harder too. I had to start assessing how neccessary it might or might not be to go into another room. I couldn't afford to go into an unnecessary one. I could get stuck at any moment, so I just stayed in the one room all day, making do with what was there. I don't actually have a way of accurately describing how the months of March and April 2013 went, because it was so frustrating and scary. My parents began to get more worried. Fights began springing out of nowhere, and ending in Mom going out for a cigarette on the bench outside, and Dad and I yelling at each other.

Going to school became harder. I found it extremely difficult to avoid the cracks between the tiles. The whole of my school is decorated in the colour blue. I guess it is a nice, communal colour for a school, but it was hell for me. At least the floors were green. I liked green. In Maths class and Business Studies class it was hard to concentrate. I was so scared of the number 4 that I was doing compulsions left, right and centre for the whole class. I didn't learn too much during those months, which was great fun when we had tests (!).

✦

Soon, OCD became practically the only thing my family talked about. Whenever we went on car trips, whenever we went shopping, the conversation always turned to what was turning out to be the most distressing situation in our lives.

Once, when Mom was having a night out with the girls, and Dad and I were going to our relation's house, it was all we talked about in the car. Dad told me he had done some research on OCD and he felt there was a good chance I had it. He told me about the compulsions he had when he was small and how he stopped them. We both agreed that we'd just have to wait until the doctor called before speculating.

Now, all we were doing was waiting to get the call from the doctor to tell us when to come in. It was just a guessing game when that would happen. Days felt like weeks. Everything moved really slowly and the OCD was always getting worse.

28/3/2013

I thought today would an unlucky day because it's the 28th., but somehow it was wonderful! I am so flipping grateful for today! I started by being cheesed off by my rituals, but my Mom snapped me out of it by thrusting a vacuum cleaner at me and then, later, making me cook dinner. Dad was outside trying to unblock the pipes leading to two of our three toilets. It's not the most glamorous job ever. He struggled through that on his own, forgetting he had a brand new pipe unblocker in the boot of his car.

My cousin is back from Australia for good, and he and my Auntie came for a visit. After hearing all the stories of bugs and heatwaves and animals, I can safely say I would not be the first person to board a flight to Australia.

My OCD interfered as usual, but I was able to put it to the back of my mind today.

Grandad came over for a while and then we watched a funny show on TV. I'm going over to my friend Sylvia's house tomorrow, so that'll be fun. I go there a lot and it never gets old.

Yesterday seemed horrible because my OCD ruined everything. Let's hope tomorrow is as easy as today.

I'm getting increasingly nervous as Easter is coming. With any celebration comes people drinking alcohol. But I guess I'll just have to get over it. I mean, there's no other solution, is there?

I'm really grateful for today. It was awesome, even though it was just an ordinary day. My compulsions were not nearly as bad and, even though I did some, I got through them quickly and I didn't get too many thoughts. I haven't felt so much desperation in a while. I may sound like a whiner, but it's the truth.

I still didn't get a call from the doctor but the sentences that I've written have no multiples of four in them, so, all in all, my mind has given me a much-needed break today.

Thank goodness for that anyway.

It was just before Easter 2013, and I was really nervous because I knew the routine over the next couple of weeks would be unpredictable, and because there would be alcohol. I kept myself busy watching the Teen Choice Awards on TV, but I couldn't help feeling horribly anxious all the time. I keep repeating that, I know, but it never went away.

My relatives came over in the afternoon, and would be staying for dinner. I was out in the kitchen, repeatedly cleaning my laptop with little spectacle wipes. It wasn't a compulsion, I just needed to do something. I was happy to get Easter eggs, but I really didn't feel like chocolate. When dinner was ready, I began counting. Counting the drinks that were passed around the table; counting the minutes it took to drink half the drink, then three quarters; constantly deliberating tipping the bottle over accidentally on purpose. I checked the volume of alcohol percentage on the bottle and began calculating. I felt cold and shivery.

Even on a normal, structured day, it was hard to do anything in my own house, as it was covered in wood knots and the colour blue, but now there were added complications, as the number 4 seemed to be mentioned in every third sentence the adults spoke. I had to keep hiding behind the laptop so they wouldn't see me tapping my nose and blowing it all away.

Later, we all went up to my Nana and Grandad's house. I sat on the couch reading, while the others were drinking. I lifted my legs a little off the ground so I wouldn't touch the tiled floor cracks. I tried to not look around too much, not wanting to trigger my OCD by seeing something blue or a wood knot. I got that cold, shivery, panicky feeling inside the moment I saw that nobody was drinking tea, just alcohol. My mind grabbed hold of that thought and twisted it into a dark, scary film scene. This made the compulsions even worse.

Every time someone laughed, every time a joke was told, every time somebody got up to get a drink, a knife of fear stabbed me in the back. I was scared they were having too much fun. I was scared that the fun was alcohol-induced. I tried to concentrate on my book, but I couldn't get into the story. I was constantly counting, keeping an eye on the drink intake, worrying. In fact, they drank very little, but I was convinced that one or two drinks would make you drunk and out of control.

When we got back to our own house, we crowded into the sitting room, and I clutched my mercifully distracting games console, praying to God it wouldn't run out of charge. My Dad got home from work and was drinking tea, so I was relieved. Everyone else only had a beer or two, but I still got incredibly anxious. I counted all the hours it would take before the alcohol stopped affecting their minds. Thoughts kept rushing through my head. I was panicking.

✦

21/4/2013

A lot is happened since I wrote here last. A LOT.

Easter has passed, and it wasn't the most fun event ever. I got so nervous when we got back to my house from Nana's and people started drinking again, I started pulling my hair out. Clumps of it, pulling away at my head until there was a bald patch on the right side. I hid all the hair in my pocket. I don't know what I was trying to achieve by tearing my hair out like that, but it felt like a small release of anxiety. Later on, when Mom wouldn't do my nightly ritual correctly, I started crying, because I was so scared. Babyish, huh?

After going to bed, I found I couldn't sleep, so I started crying and ranting to myself about why I was so scared. My mouth was opening and closing, just whispering the words. I repeated how sorry I was for seeming ungrateful fwhen everyone was so kind to me, for acting so crazily on a day that was supposed to be happy. I went through the whole tirade, rattling on about anything I could think of to keep myself distracted, hoping I would come to some sort of conclusion as to why this was happening. It was like some sort of fever had gripped me and wouldn't let me go. I was speaking half to God, half to whatever was out there that was causing this episode. My mind kept racing as I prayed and ranted. It was crazy.

A few days later, after the bald patch had sprouted little stubbly bits, the doctor called. It was a Wednesday.

I remember my Dad answering the phone and going out into the utility room. Mom and I were listening in silence. I lost complete interest in the short movie I was going to make that afternoon.

As soon as the phone was hung up, we all crowded round to hear what the doctor had to say. It turns out it wasn't the doctor. It was the therapist.

I didn't know the difference then. They were all the same, I thought. My Dad had told him all of the compulsions I did and all the fears I had.

I didn't know the therapist's name or age or anything, but It didn't matter. An appointment was set up for Friday to determine whether or not I had OCD. I was really relieved at that, but also nervous. How was it going to go? If I did have OCD, what then? It was scary. I was really grateful to my parents for believing me when I said I thought I had it, but I was dreading what was going to happen next.

Chapter Four
Diagnosis

21/4/2013

I was diagnosed as having OCD by a man named Mr Collins, who's a specialist in CBT, so I guess you could call him a therapist. I have a separate doctor too, named Dr McGovern. They're both really nice, but I am really shy talking about this kind of stuff.

I remember the morning before I went to the Medical Centre with my parents. My Dad said it might be useful to write down a list of my compulsions, fears and obsessions before going, so I could show it to Mr Collins. I remember being scared, but also kind of excited. It was an icy April morning, and I ran around with my dog Shadow and cat Marshmallow to distract myself while my parents drank coffee in the kitchen. We were all wondering what was going to happen. When it was time to go, we bundled into the car and set off.

When I saw the Medical Centre, that sharp knife of fear struck me once more. Walking in, I realised the whole place smelled too healthy, too communal, and too medical. I looked down at the floor, my gaze's usual focus to hide from other triggers.

"You've got to be kidding me."

The floor in the medical centre was a dark blue linoleum, with navy pieces scattered around for effect, I guess. It certainly had an effect on me.

Of course. The medical profession is obsessed with blue. Blue clipboards. Blue name tags, blue pens for the cranky receptionists, blue plasters for the kids who fell off their trampolines.

When my Dad saw the state of the floor, he burst out laughing. "Rebecca, you're screwed!"

I glared at him and darkened my voice in mock disgust, "The universe is testing me," which earned laughs from Mom.

I must have looked like a lunatic, walking through that hallway, with my head pointed straight up at the white ceiling tiles. I can only imagine what the reception ladies must have thought when they saw a teenager walking past the consultation window, head pointed at such an abnormal and seemingly uncomfortable angle, fully focused on the ceiling. My parents stopping briefly by their window saying that we were going upstairs. There are only two medical service rooms upstairs: the general nurse's office and the mental health room.

They didn't have to be Psychic Sally to take a wild guess as to where I was headed.

We waited on the squashy couches outside the door upstairs. I was jumping out of my skin at this point. I couldn't sit still and I didn't really feel like playing with toy cars, so I decided to explore. I quickly found there were only a few rooms upstairs: the nurse's office, the bathroom, the therapist's room and the break room. There was an odd-looking old-fashioned radio spitting out unfitting tunes. We spent our time looking at the psychiatry poster on the wall. Minutes seemed to go by like hours. Everything we had discussed at length for months and had inched our way towards was now here in front of us. It was actually happening, and that was crazy. I felt like it was all my fault that we ended up here. And it was.

After an eternity, we could hear footsteps on the stairs. I began to feel sick. A man appeared carrying a clipboard and files, wearing a little ID tag around his neck. I automatically stood up, but my legs felt like jelly. Mr Collins introduced himself and unlocked the room next to the psychiatry poster.

Inside, I saw with big fluffy chairs with hairy cushions, a coffee table and a counter with a sink. On it was an ancient bottle of water I wouldn't trust to be safe to drink. There were pamphlets nudged into every corner. A bunch of CDs and a player were stuck at the side, and the windows looked out onto the car park. There were pens and booklets on the windowsill, and a crooked picture frame, which I couldn't reach to straighten.

Naturally, Dad took the biggest comfy seat because, well, he's Dad, while Mom and I perched on the other chairs. Mr Collins put his clipboard and files onto the table. They weren't straight, but that was the least of my anxieties at that moment. I did my best to ignore it, as I couldn't bear to straighten something in front on a stranger, even if I was hurting. We began talking.

We introduced ourselves. I was Rebecca, age thirteen, from the countryside. Mr Collins said he was named Michael or Mick and he was a psychiatric nurse. I thought of Mick dressed in a nurse's outfit and I nearly burst out laughing. I sometimes forget men can also be nurses. I didn't know at all what a psychiatric one was, but after a few bemused questions I found out it was a nurse that worked in psychiatric hospitals. He was also an expert in CBT (Cognitive Behavioural Therapy).

Then we got to the topic at hand: OCD. He asked a bunch of questions. We had to go through our family history of illnesses and other things. Some unexpected stories of habits running through my family surfaced. From Dad's comments to Mick, I learned more about his childhood 'habits'.

We were asked questions, such as, "Does any other member of your family have any mental health issues?" and, "Are you currently taking any kind of drug?" He didn't think we took drugs, it's just routine for diagnosis to get the full background, even if the person diagnosing the patient has a predetermined idea.

"YES SIR! I DRANK FIFTY BOTTLES OF VODKA AND DOWNED A WHOLE BOTTLE OF SEVEN SEAS COD LIVER OIL VITAMINS AND I'M FEELING ALIVE."

I didn't dare say that though.

We had to go through this description of my Dad's habits, my habits and how they affected me, go through all the family history and everything.

Shortly after he moved here from America when he was thirteen, he began tapping things a certain number of times because it didn't feel 'right' otherwise. He would avoid the wood knots in the floor just like I did. Maybe there is a genetic factor to this thing. Mom says she's never met any two people as alike as myself and Dad.

My aunt would make fun of him for that, but he always tried to keep it secret. He'd probably have gotten a brick thrown at him or something if anyone had noticed. Back then, if you didn't work fast or hard enough, you were pulled up on it very quickly. I didn't know much about our family history of illness. It's not the type of thing you'd bring up over Christmas dinner. Well, I would, but it's not generally acceptable.

When I was asked talk about myself, I was extremely hesitant. I wasn't even sure how to sit while talking about this kind of stuff. I couldn't look him in the eye for more than two seconds and had to talk to the coffee table. The top of the coffee table. My gaze followed down the legs to the floor and ... it was blue.

I had to describe a typical day for me, but I only got as far as the end of the morning when the conversation turned. I was asked how long I'd had habits, what age was I when I first got them and all this stuff. It was weird. You know that feeling you get when you're in the middle of a really nervy situation and you can feel your head racing? That's what it was like discussing something so secret with someone I didn't know very well.

It felt surreal, sitting there, purposely distracting myself by clawing the decorative button on my coat, while spewing out thoughts that didn't seem half as bad when said aloud. Finally when he finished scribbling God knows what onto the little (red!) clipboard and put it down, he said, "Well, I think you have a form of OCD."

Oh. Well.

No big shocker there, huh? I knew it anyway, but I didn't know what to think when he actually came out with it.

My parents were nodding away, concentrating on everything he said about treatments for OCD, and also told about how it operated, like I didn't know that already. A person gets bad thoughts and does rituals to stop them. One theory is that I don't have enough *serotonin* in my brain. Serotonin is a sort of happy chemical. If you don't have enough of it, you may get obsessive thoughts. Sometimes, a lack of it can cause depression. Medication can give your brain the extra serotonin it needs, but that is not the first line of treatment. OCD can also be addressed using therapy.

Mr Collins said there are three steps to treating OCD. Number One: Cognitive Behavioural Therapy, or CBT. Number Two: Medication with CBT. Number Three: Hospital. Later on, you'll find out I had to have number two, even though my Mom and Dad kept telling me they'd use number three, which scared the crap out of me.

One night I was doing compulsions so intensely that my Mom came in and sat down beside me. She was too quiet, so I asked if she was sad with regard to the hospital. She said, "No", but that she was worried. I asked her if I was going to a hospital. She said, "Yes, no, I don't know". It was scary. I took the hospital thing seriously. I told my parents I'd run away if they tried to take me. Dad said they could run faster and catch me. I said I'd never go. Dad laughed scornfully and said they'd take me anyway. He said the 'men in white coats' were coming for me. Thanks Dad.

Over the next few days, I began reading up on OCD and CBT, although I knew most of it anyway. I was thinking, "Okay, great. Thanks for the diagnosis I already know. Now what are the magic words that'll stop this crap?" I was lazy. I thought things would be done for me.

I had my OCD in my head all the time. Not just the symptoms, but the fact that I could now call it OCD. I was angry at my parents for no reason. I felt that if they had taken me to a doctor when they saw me making peculiar noises and rolling my eyes back when I was younger, I might have actually been able to get this problem sorted out sooner. But that was selfish and horrible of me, so I tried to avoid that train of thought.

An appointment was made for the next week with Mr Collins for my first session of CBT. I read that therapists talk, you talk, and the tiniest things you say will be picked up and reveal what you are actually thinking and going through. They ask questions constructively to make you think and realise things yourself. They try to help you change the way you think about things, so you can fight on your own. You become immersed in your own story until you can see your own solutions.

It sounds truly brilliant. Better than any medication. It will set you on the right path, if you'll let it.

I didn't.

Chapter Five
Defiance

When I first started Cognitive Behavioural Therapy, it was great fun getting off school, but not always, since I sometimes had to go on school half-days as well, and those were the days I liked to hang out with friends. I couldn't tell them where I was going. I didn't know how they'd react to it. It was not that big of a deal, really, but when they are all gathered around a coffee table eating vinegar-coated chips and laughing at old text messages, it's not the time to bring up stuff like that.

I didn't know what to expect from therapy. I didn't really know whether the sessions I was going to were CBT or not. There was nobody saying, "This is officially CBT". They were just talking, and I was I responding. I was still shy as heck with Mr Collins. I had to discuss my rituals with him and what I felt would happen if I didn't do them, and that was stuff I'd never even said out loud.

We discussed different topics each time, yet they all centred on OCD in some way. I was given questionnaires to complete, ticking things from a list of anxiety triggers. Once, sitting outside in the hallway to complete one of these, I found that the pen wasn't working, but I decided to circle the answers by pressing hard on the paper so that my responses were visible from the impressions left by the dried-up ballpoint. I thought I was being proactive, but when I presented it to Mick, he gave me a working pen and I had to do it again.

On a typical day at CBT, my parents would sit beside me, Mr Collins across from us, and we'd chat about our day. I'd find out more about him and he'd find out more about me. Once in a while we'd run slightly off topic, speaking about something of mutual interest, but he'd always snap right back to the root of the conversation. The OCD.

"So, how are we doing?" would probably be the opening sentence.

"Well, I'm good."

I'd tell him about the past week I had, what I did on the weekdays, and any other news. I was extremely fidgety and shy. I would play with all the buttons on my coat and the hairy cover of the armchair. We'd go through loads of different topics – more like having a chat with a friend. It was not really what I would have expected therapy to be like.

I actually found it kind of fun there. I occasionally made him laugh and he made me laugh too. And ... he watches Big Bang Theory. When he told me that I knew we would get on great.

We'd go through loads of different topics – more like a chat than what I would have expected therapy to be.

I was becoming accustomed to talking. I was perfectly happy with the idea that somehow, this talking would make me better in my unconscious mind. I went there week after week, enjoying my hour-long session with Mr. Collins, thinking, "Great, I'm getting better every time I come here!"

It wasn't all roses though. I began to understand that he wasn't asking these questions in order to get my opinion. I was meant to GET RID of the compulsions. There came the day where I had to stop talking and start doing. I realised that I couldn't be lazy. I needed to make an effort. Even therapy has some discipline to it. I was asked to rate my compulsions from Easiest-to-Resist to Hardest-to-Resist. I chose symmetry as being the easiest. We talked about symmetry and how it was affecting my life and how I think I could stop it.

He introduced me to ERP: Exposure and Response Prevention. That means you expose a person to something they fear, but don't let them do a compulsion. It's like telling a person with germ OCD to touch a toilet seat and not wash their hands. The aim of this was to get the person so familiar with the anxiety that it would no longer faze them and they would finally break free of the shackles. For me, it might involve making an item crooked, leaving it for 5 seconds and then straightening it. If practised enough, that length of time could get longer and longer.

With ERP, I wouldn't just be set a task, and then shooed out of the room to complete it, my parents would participate too, helping me to expose myself to the compulsion, in this case, the urge to straighten everything.

I was terrified by this concept. I wasn't just scared of the possible (imaginary) repercussions of not having something straight.

✦

We had this whole plan set out, with my parent's involvement. They remarked on my progress and interjected as much as they could, and soon a road ahead was paved. I seemed to be stuck in the potholes though, because I wouldn't try.

I would go home after CBT with a new task in hand, and engage in cowardly procrastination. I would put off the ERP until later and when it was later it would be tomorrow. My parents would remind me about it, but I would snap at them and tell them I'd do it later.

Truth is, I was secretly terrified that I'd start to lose my OCD. I tried so many times to make myself stop wanting to hang on to it, but the feeling kept getting stronger. I told myself, "No, you don't want OCD. Nobody wants it, and you don't either." I wasn't even aware I was being selfish, wasting my parent's time and good money, and secretly knowing it was to no avail. They'd keep trying to make me do ERP, hopelessly unaware I wasn't just scared of the obsession, but also of losing it. They'd make me do it, but I knew it wasn't going to help at all.

I felt like I had a fault in my DNA. I had ridiculous thoughts and I wasn't sure why. I kept trying to correct these thoughts by telling myself I was just confused, but the OCD kept getting in my face, insisting it wanted to stay.

I felt crazier than I have ever felt in my life, like I was losing my mind. Why does every other OCD person want rid of it, and not me? Maybe I subconsciously lied to the therapist and I have been misdiagnosed with OCD! All these thoughts were spinning around in my head, and I was freaking out.

It was such a blurry, maze-like whirlwind of thought, I wasn't sure how to escape, so I decided to do nothing. Half of me kept up the pretence, telling myself I wanted to do the CBT, but the other half was stopping me, so I ignored both halves and just let myself drift along with the tide.

It wasn't a completely conscious choice to cop out like that. It was a more desperate decision in response to a fragmented point of view. If it had been possible for someone to chart out my whole situation clearly like a map, I might have been able to make clear choices – I might have been less muddled. But it was a very muddled few months.

It was during March and April that I had two particularly bad OCD episodes that came out of nowhere.

One morning, it was apparent from the moment I woke up that it was going to be a bad day. I knew it. Sometimes, with OCD, you just know. It took me longer to get dressed, to do my dance for the doorways, to hop the squares in the bathroom, to tap my nose and blow away all the bad colours, numbers and words in the world around me. It took me twenty-five minutes to brush my teeth and another fifteen to get downstairs. I can't remember exactly, but it took me even longer to eat my breakfast and, when it came to getting out of the house, I couldn't.

Sitting having breakfast, all I saw was wood knots. Everything that ever triggered me was magnified that day. The world was covered in anxiety-inducing colours and numbers, and my thoughts raced.

I no longer went out the front door because I needed to avoid the hall as best I could, so it was normal for me to go out the patio door around the back, but before doing this, I had to get the 'overall' ritual done. The overall ritual meant that I had to go through all the rooms I'd been in that day and tap my nose and blow away all the bad colours, numbers, words or wood knots I saw or heard, all in one go, with one breath for each category of 'bad' thing. I had to do this immediately before leaving the house. It's like applying hand sanitiser. You're germ-free now, until the germs come again. You have to leave before they do. I had to leave the house immediately after the overall ritual before getting triggered again, just like the germs invading and ultimately overriding the hand sanitiser.

But today, I couldn't seem to get the overall ritual right. Sometimes it might take me a little longer to get it done, but not usually enough to stop me from going to school. Mom might get a bit narked and I may get frustrated, but we'd always get out. Not today.

I kept spotting something else that would trigger me and would then have to restart the process. It didn't help that I was being told to hurry up, though you can't blame a patient parent for trying to speed things along.

After about an hour and a half of trying, I was slumped against the wall and Mom had a cigarette in her hand. It became clear that neither of us had any intention of going anywhere. I had missed assembly anyway. I could have gone in, but I was past trying. I had worn myself and my mother out.

My chest was aching from doing all those breathing rituals and I couldn't start all over again. I had to just skip school that day. I know it seems like a weak way out, but we were both exhausted. We only just about made it to school on 'normal' days. Mom called them and told them I was sick and wouldn't be coming in. I sure was sick. Sick with OCD.

I spent the rest of the day in one room, the kitchen, to minimise rituals. I went on the computer, which was proving a dangerous haven for me during these times, and tried to make a movie. It involved my cat Marshmallow's adventures through the kitchen. He wasn't very cooperative.

Later, I transferred to the sitting room. I took my computer with me and stayed on it all evening. When it was bedtime, I lifted my leg to go higher than everything in the room, and did various other rituals on the radiator, double doors, couch, hallway, stairs, hallway, couch, double doors, radiator. I got none of them right, and kept having to restart.

When I went up to my bedroom, I had to do the ritual for the door, the wood, the colours, the symmetry, everything. I didn't get to use the time I usually have before lights out. Mom came up later to find me in the position I had been an hour and a half before, a large red mark showing where I had been tapping my nose furiously, and my head doing the 'rolling around' ritual like a demented dervish. I did my ten-minute long set of ritualistic prayers and tried to fall asleep. I wish I could say I am exaggerating.

The other day I was off school played out basically the same way as that one. Not for one minute was anybody in my house lazy about putting in the effort, but we were all burned out like an overused motor, like the CD drive Dad says will break if I keep my Sims game in there too long.

It was hell, but STILL I wasn't sure I wanted to be free of it. That didn't seem such an unreasonable viewpoint back then.

✦

21/4/2013

I got to meet Dr McGovern at my CBT session. She's very nice. She asked me questions such as, "Are you worried about your mental health?" and, "What do you think would happen if you had to take medication?" which are pretty odd questions to a thirteen year-old.

Medication? NO WAY! I do NOT want medication! As for the mental health thing, I am a little freaked out. I'm able to think about OCD logically and all NOW, but I feel like I'm going crazy. I know I'm not crazy, and this may seem stupid, but when I'm grown up and living away from home in the future, if I still have this, I won't have anyone to motivate me, and I'll get worse.

Everything was dull and grey. It felt like time was passing without me.

I was trying to figure out why I wanted OCD and how to stop wanting it, so that contributed to my little whinge here.

It's time I hitched up my skirt and stopped acting ridiculous. When I get a 'sorry' moment, I'll just have to snap myself out of it. It is getting more difficult though, and I can't really tell what is ridiculous and what's not anymore.

In other news, I'm going to CBT on Friday, which means I get out of double Science yet again! On the downside, I haven't been trying too hard to get rid of my symmetry stuff and now it may result in me taking medication. I AM NOT TAKING MEDICATION! That's for crazy people!

I know the doctor is insisting that it's the way forward, and that the CBT option on its own is not showing solid enough results, so I really should be making more of an effort. Damn it.

But, as anyone knows, medication messes you up. You could get crazily addicted to it. Plus, you might get it in a needle and I DON'T WANT TO BE INJECTED THANK YOU VERY MUCH!

They can't physically force me. They'll never do that. It's against the flipping law!

26/4/2013

Today I went to another glorious session of CBT. Whoopee!

Mainly we discussed involving me in some sort of social thing so I can be less attached to my parents. They are scouring the county for something I could do to take my mind off OCD. Another thing that freaked me out was another discussion about medication. YET AGAIN. I told the doctor all the reasons why I SHOULDN'T take it, from brain damage to addiction, I don't care how crazy the excuse sounded, I'd say anything that could stop me taking it. He explained again how it could help me. I didn't agree.

Everyone around me is telling me I'm getting worse and worse, but I'm not! I'm fine! I just have a lot of habits! That's all! I'm not getting any worse. Sure, I may get a little nervous from time to time, but that can't be helped, can it? NOPE. They're trying their best, but they don't realise I'm the only one who can control it. They will never be inside my head, therefore they are powerless. So just give up already.

One of the worst things about being in the Medical Centre is that the floors are a deep blue. It's HARD to climb a flight of stairs when you are either staring at the ceiling or tapping your nose and puffing. There's an old radio outside the break room and a few rooms for the nurses (I got a lollipop from one!), and inside the break room there are tables and chairs and magazines and a tin of Fox's biscuits in deep purple with the panda called Vinnie on the front. He has a Bronx accent, which my Dad used to have before he moved back to Ireland.

Anyway I am adamant that I will never take medication. No tablets or injections or anything! I'm sorry if I'm overreacting and I should be open to suggestions about stuff that might actually work, but I really don't want it!

I have one week left to prove I can improve on my own, OR ELSE!

I'm not taking anything!

… except for compliments …

In other news, this fitness instructor guy came into our school to do a presentation. It was fun, because we got out of class! He even had this odd little chart telling us how to 'read' our urine to see if we're hydrated. We did a vigorous exercise to all these really loud, euphoric pop songs. I am pooped! I'm going now. BYE-BYE!

28/4/2013

Well, yesterday turned out to be completely dark. I went to town with Mom, got given out to for my rituals, was reminded that everyone was staring at me, and all in all, it was a wonderful day –NOT!

I'm getting scared. Everyone is serious about me taking this medicine thing. I am just as serious. I can either take the dangerous medicine, or fix myself on my own. Both options are equally hard, so I guess there is no easy way out.

My parents and I were in the sitting room, and the conversation turned to OCD. This happens often now, almost every night. My Dad suddenly paused the TV and asked me without any warning how I planned to get rid of it. I either mumbled something or said nothing, coupled with a dirty look for each. Usually after a question like this, the TV would resume and we'd all act normal again, but this time, he wouldn't let it go.

"Rebecca, do you like your OCD?"

"No."

"Then why won't you try?"

"I don't want to."

"Why not?"

"Because it's not that bad!"

"Are you kidding me? Yes it is!"

"It is NOT!"

"We've forked over money to a doctor for you to stop this OCD!"

"I KNOW!"

"Then why won't you just TRY?"

"I WILL!"

"When?"

"I DON'T KNOW!"

All this time, my mind was screaming at me, "Don't you dare try! You WANT your OCD!

Of course I didn't say this, because they had enough to deal with, so I kept my mouth shut and continued my pretence as being someone who wanted their OCD gone. It didn't seem like such a selfish deception.

Dad said, "We want you to leave that remote control crooked, wait five seconds, and then you can straighten it."

Needless to say, I hesitated. I continued to refuse until things got a bit heated.

My special markers I use to draw comics were lined up by colour under the coffee table. I had been fiddling with them during the interrogation. Finally, my Dad leapt up, grabbed two markers and held them up in the air above his head before I could stop him.

"Very funny. Can I have them back now?"

Denied.

I began chasing him, running around the sitting room, clawing at him to give them back. He refused, holding them high as he could. I jumped on him, I grabbed him, screamed and cried at him. My anxiety was going through the roof and it was turning into rage as well. We were all shouting. Mom had this terrible worried look on her face. I was raging. Dad wouldn't give the markers back until I promised to do the CBT. I was attacking my Dad over some asymmetrical markers. It looked like a circus act. It was a circus act.

He finally got tired of dancing around the room with my beloved markers and made me promise to move the remote control. I promised, gratefully grabbing the markers back so I could hurriedly put them back into their straightened, colour-coded position. Dad sat back down. Mom still had the same expression on her face.

I purposely took an extra-long time to straighten them, my parents watching me, because I wanted to put off the ERP task for as long as I could. Eventually, they copped on, and I had to finish with the markers.

Even still, I was trying to figure out how I could get out of moving the bloody remote control. My parents were patient for an extremely long while, sitting in their chairs, missing their TV shows, just to watch me do something a two year-old could do. They were very nice and encouraging, but even their patience wore thin after forty-five minutes of watching their kid staring at a black zapper.

So they again started insisting that I nudge it, even threatening to call Mairéad (Dr McGovern) to bring over the medication straight away. There was something sad in their voices which was worse than anger. "It's plain that you just can't help yourself ... "

This was panic stations. They were SERIOUS. It wasn't like those childhood times when, if I misbehaved, Mom would mock-seriously threaten to call the police to take me away. She was joking then, but not now.

Just when Dad rose from his chair, sighing that he was now going to call the doctor, I grabbed the remote and shoved it crooked.

"One ... Two ... " My parents counted slowly. My OCD was telling me they counted way too slowly to spite me. I glowered at the remote control, sitting there, in all its stupid asymmetrical glory while time slowed to a crawl. I wanted to scream.

"Four ... Five ... YAY!" I jumped to straighten it.

My parents started cheering and I just fell on Dad, crying. We just hugged and hugged. They were saying, "Well done!" to me over and over again. I felt great that I made them happy, but secretly horrified that I could be losing my OCD, and guilty that I even felt that way.

I was acting happy, but it wasn't real.

It was like that Irish guy who went into the Big Brother TV show last year, pretending to be somebody he's not to fool the housemates. I was fooling everybody, but it was getting me nowhere.

Chapter Six
Parents

If I'm going to be writing about my life with OCD, I must refer to my parents. Because it's not just 'my life' with OCD, it's theirs as well. I don't want it to be theirs, but it has affected all of us. They have felt the brunt of it, and, without my parents' sympathy and patience, I would never have told anybody, and it wouldn't ever have been diagnosed.

In many ways, they have been affected by it just as deeply, because they were always left to speculate on its severity. I knew myself what my OCD was like, as I was the one experiencing it, so I was kind of initiated into the whole thing. I was used to it, and I found my own levels of comfort. My parents were living on the outside, the 'normal' side, where no behaviour is altered to make life feel 'right', where they could do whatever they wanted. They had to watch their kid living a crazy, restricted lifestyle, doing ridiculous rituals.

I wished that they could be with me 'inside' OCD and see that it was okay sometimes. If only they could have been in my mind when things were ok. If only they didn't have to worry unnecessarily. I adjusted to new levels of comfort all the time and forgot about old ones. It wasn't all bad.

Please stop worrying about me.

I'm worrying about you worrying about me worrying about you.

And that's worrying.

My parents have a big thing about not coddling children. They tell me I will not be coddled, and I am perfectly capable of taking care of myself. That is not to say that my household is uncaring. Far from it. If you are feeling sick, you are taken seriously. You are hugged and cuddled and given medicine, like in any other home.

But physical symptoms are a lot easier to empathise with than mental ones. I can see why. When a person gets a rash, you can see the person is not lying or looking for attention. It's there. You can see it. The person is ill. With mental or behavioural symptoms, you cannot tell whether the person is acting up for attention or is really unwell. Nobody knows about mental illness like they do physical illness. My parents had heard of OCD, but they were initially quite sceptical.

They were inclined towards the common belief that OCD is a hypochondriac illness, which many people find easier to accept than the 'politically incorrect' fact that it is a mental health issue. If there's one thing my household laughs the most at, it's political correctness. So basically, if you're not fatally wounded or sneezing vomit, you're fine.

So when I was four, and giving my Mom a toy every day before school so I wouldn't have a bad day, and crying at the school gate, they thought I was just adjusting to a new school. When I was seven, and gulping and holding my breath repeatedly, my parents thought I was just a kid being a kid. When I was eleven, and constantly swirled my head around and around in a crazy pattern, they shrugged and didn't take much notice. Mom thought I had tics and would grow out of them.

So, I watched OCD programmes on TV. When I was nine or ten, I Googled it, and, as the online medical definition came up, I just cried.

And then, I forgot about it. For three years. I guess I just didn't care, or it wasn't at the forefront of my priorities at that time. It hadn't grown up yet. But it did grow up, and when I first noticed it, it (if it doesn't sound too dramatic) was spiralling out of control. It was only when I turned thirteen that I was finally old enough to realise that, in the words of Miss Clavel from Madeline, "Something is not right!"

My parents always believe me when I tell them something, because they know I'm trustworthy. And I am. I don't tell lies. But sometimes, a person can tell innocent fibs without even realising it. They exaggerate. The root idea may be true, but they embellish the facts to make it seem more important or serious than it really is. These people can be called gossips or drama queens, or just thought of as being over-analytical.

I think my parents found it hard to accept I wasn't a drama queen. I am in some respects, but when it came to telling them about the severity of my OCD, I stuck to the raw truth – that it was extremely hard to concentrate at school, that I found it hard to talk to my friends and that I constantly felt anxious.

Sure, all teenagers have problems, but when does it cross the line?

My Mom suggested various reasons for this anxiety. Was someone bullying me at school? Was I nervous about exams? Could I pinpoint the cause of the anxiety at all? No, I couldn't. It just came. I explained it was extremely hard to control it. It was then that we sought a diagnosis.

I am grateful that they took it seriously. I am really happy with that. I found that being honest is great, because you don't end up like 'the boy who cried wolf' when something really does go wrong. But even after appointments with a doctor and therapist, I felt like my parents thought of this treatment as a 'new way to fix an old problem.' My issues may have been cleared up faster and dealt with differently if I had been part of an older generation, where nothing but exemplary behaviour would be tolerated. I would soon have had those habits knocked out of me.

Perhaps. Maybe it would have made me more resistant to OCD. Back then though, it wouldn't have been acknowledged. Maybe taking a kid to the psychiatrist is now the 'done thing' for behavioural issues affecting this new, soft generation of technology-obsessed kids. It's the newer, 'lite' version of a good spanking. Maybe, in 'the old days' kids were so involved in hard work they didn't have time for thoughts or compulsions. Perhaps I was just under-occupied.

It was hard for my parents to accept that I couldn't do many of the things I wanted to. My life was severely impacted, and they couldn't figure out why I was putting up with it. I was always so good at standing up to bullies, so why should this be any different? They learned to appreciate that the answer to that question is that bullying is not a stand-alone illness. OCD *is* an illness, and one which is very difficult to identify, and to distinguish from 'tics' and 'acting up'.

It took them a while to come to terms with the fact that OCD was a real mental illness, and not just a dubious label. Even when they started to believe that I really could be in trouble, I think they still had the hope that I could kick this on my own without medical help.

Back when Dad had his compulsions, he used to flap his hands before opening a door, or circle his feet around the dents in the floor just like me. That suggested to me that anybody can have OCD, even in a strict family such as his, where being silly is not tolerated. The difference is, his compulsions did not last long. My Dad was sick and tired of being laughed at and of his mind telling him stupid things, so he just swore at it, ignored the urges and got on with his business.

Maybe that's why my parents found it difficult to see me succumbing to something similar to what my Dad had dealt with on his own. I have his way of thinking, his temperament (from my Mom I got the bushy eyebrows). My role as the weak kid getting bullied on the playground was unfathomable to him. None of us had ever seen me as that child. Heck, when I was nine, I threw a chair at someone who annoyed me.

Succumbing to OCD is like being that weak kid getting beaten up for lunch money at school. I had always been taught to take no crap, but here I was, taking it.

There were days when difficult situations would arise at home. The confusion and frustration had bubbled up to a certain level in my parents' minds and now it was boiling over.

There were times when Mom had to go sit outside by herself because she couldn't stand being in the sitting room, looking at me repeating, repeating, repeating. Or when Dad and I had loud outbursts and arguments about how I wouldn't try, with him telling me, "God wouldn't like this." Times when Mom screamed at me about the numbing tensions that had taken over in recent months, or when Dad stormed out of the house telling me I was going to kill the entire family with this stress. How I should "enjoy the funeral" while I'm at it. Looking at me straight in the eye. Said with such conviction, like he really hated me. But no, he didn't hate me. He hated the OCD. He just found it hard to separate the two, sometimes.

Parents may think it's just their kids being kids. There is no reason for them to automatically chalk up every bit of odd behaviour to a specific illness, but imagine if there was a world where everybody knew symptoms of mental illness as well as they did physical ones.

That's why we have to spread the word about OCD and that it is as much a threatening illness as many well-known physical ones. Mental health should be part of a routine check-up. So that parents know. So kids are believed and can get the help they need.

OCD is not a quirk of personality.

My parents are fantastic people and I love them to bits. I'm sure they didn't expect a kid with OCD, but I'm grateful they took it on board and helped me. Sometimes I wish OCD never happened, but it did and I've learned a lot from it.

I want to say sorry to my parents for the worry and stress I caused them; for the fallout. Parents and family in general, whether related by blood or not, are a big part of recovery from illnesses such as OCD, from being in a state of constant, patient endurance during the worst times, to celebrating during the best.

They believed me when I knew something was wrong. That's why this chapter is dedicated to them, the real heroes of OCD. I love you guys.

P.S. Please make me chicken for dinner!

Chapter Seven
School-Day Glory

He's going to die you know. Dad. With those cigarettes he smokes, he's a goner. I've seen your mother too. She thinks she knows it all. Who does she think she is, telling you everything is okay when she goes out with Dad? How could she possibly know?

Puny humans, thinking they know everything. They tell you they'll be fine before they go on a night out. That they've been doing this for years, since before you were born. They even tell you the pub they're going to, just to make sure you're not scared. They only wish you could see everything is going to be okay on their night out. Well, we only wish they could see things from our point of view, don't we, Rebecca? We can see things they can't. We can see the danger in their actions. How many films have you seen where the protagonist says, "Everything will be alright" just before the disaster? Silly parents, thinking they can go out and stay safe while doing what they want. If they say everything will be alright and not to worry, they're setting themselves up for a jinx."

It talks to me. Sometimes it wouldn't even have to give me instructions. I'd already know what to do.

I remember being so tired of compulsions in the middle of the night that I would tempt fate by thinking, "Bet you're going to make me do it again ten times." Then I'd go, "Damn it," and fight to not think about that command. Because I knew if I thought about it, it would become 'law'. But, of course, repressing thoughts doesn't work, and I would think about it anyway. It could go on like that all night. Next thing I know, it's five in the morning and I'm circling the middle of the floor of my bedroom touching the wardrobe thirty-three times and tapping my nose three times (because three's a good number). Wait, I just thought of thirty-three. Okay, now tapping my nose thirty-three times.

It was a hopeless period.

Never be definite. You'll regret it.

It keeps talking. It tells me things that make me want to scream. I don't want to hear crazy scenarios. I don't want a horror movie in my head about somebody getting slit across the throat and then the murderer infecting themselves with the person's blood to contract AIDS in an act of slow suicide. I can see the knife and the first line of blood appearing. And flowing down their neck. And the victim falling to their knees.

How detailed can you get? How long will the movie last before I can try to fall asleep? My OCD sees that as a challenge.

✦

30/4/2013

My parents ordered this book online about OCD and it came just as I was going to my cousin's Confirmation. I had a look in it. It seems really good.

I went to the dentist to have my braces adjusted. It hurt for a while, but then you get used to it. Heck, an hour later I chowed my way through two bacon sandwiches! It's fun going there, because the clinic is close to both the book and the art shops.

Today I found out I have to go to this Educational Psychologist. I'll take an IQ test. The point of that, I don't know. Dad says it'll help find strengths and weaknesses in how I learn. I have no idea what this has to do with OCD or anything, but I guess it couldn't hurt. He says everyone should get them. I find it exciting!

6/5/2013

Sylvia came over on Saturday and Róisín came over for dinner on Sunday and got to stay over until Monday, when I went to Sylvia's house! We played in the river and it was really fun! It was especially exciting because I wasn't able to get over the slippery rocks across the river until now! Her dog Daisy came too and proved very helpful when I needed to get across the river to lopsided rocks. I just grabbed onto her back and shoved my way across. Daisy seemed happy to oblige! Later on, Sylvia sent me a photo of me clinging onto a branch for dear life. It was entitled "The Bucka Expedition!"

They have a lot of yummy food over there (at Sylvia's house).

So yeah. I had an eventful weekend. See you later!

It was only after I got home after this long, fun weekend that I found out my parents reaction to what had happened on that particular Monday. I had been about to go to Sylvia's house for the river adventure. It was routine for me to go out the back door, but I couldn't seem to get it right. I couldn't get rid of the wood knots and the blue and the unstraight things in the house. I really wanted to get out, as I knew it would be great at Sylvia's, not to mention she's my best friend, but I couldn't get out the flipping door.

My parents were just sitting there, telling me to hurry up as I went through my rituals. I had forgotten to keep my eyes closed that day, so the process got delayed even further as I kept seeing my microscopic enemies floating around. That was my own stupid fault, of course.

That was a bad episode. I was over half an hour late to Sylvia's house. I knew I had disappointed my parents again. When I returned home, they insisted that I to do ERP. I resisted, and, while we were giving out to each other, it came out that Mom had been crying because of what had happened earlier. That shocked me. Parents don't cry, do they?

That shocked me into doing the ERP. I moved the remote control and waited a few seconds before straightening it and made my Mom promise, promise, promise she would never cry or get sad again, for my sake. Selfish, I know.

I was scared she was becoming depressed. That someone could be sad like that because of my problems had never occurred to me. I thought Mom was going downhill and I felt awful.

✦

I had an 'episode' at school.

My OCD behaviour was worsening at school. I never thought it would. I had this idea that everything in school would carry on the same, regardless of what happened outside.

I wish.

This is what happened:

I'm in Business Studies Class. Floor is a horrible colour. I sit down at the desk and TRY to pay attention. Many items in the room are horrible colours. Numbers in books are horrible and so is the colour of the books themselves. The words people say are horrible. I can only thank my lucky stars I'm at the very front of the class, so there is no one in front of me to turn around and see my nose-tapping superpowers.

My disorganised desk is horrible, so I organise it. I'm like a Death the Kid cosplayer. Wait, is that book really straight in line with the edge of the desk? Maybe if I straighten it – damn it, I knocked that and something else askew. Where is a ruler when you need it? Oh yeah, in my pencil case, but if I get that out, I'll have to open and shut it repeatedly and touch it again and again and pull it in and out of my bag repeatedly, but there is no guarantee I'll get it right.

All during this deliberation, I get an accidental glimpse of the floor, so I have to do a compulsion for that. Wait, did I get that right? What if I didn't?

Throughout this SECOND deliberation, I see another horrible colour. Another compulsion added to my schedule. I must do the first and second one again and again until I get it right.

Jeez, how long is this taking? I glance at the clock and freeze. Classic rookie mistake. DO NOT LOOK AT THE CLOCK. BAD NUMBERS ON THAT CLOCK. 4, 8, 12, even 2 hurts if it's a bad day.

"OCD, I CHOOSE YOU!" I shout as I throw my custom Pokéball at the clock.

Just kidding.

I perform the nose tapping compulsion again. I keep thinking what the other kids might be seeing.

As I look away from the clock, I realise I may not have nose-tapped right, or I might have accidentally breathed in inadvertantly. DO IT AGAIN. DO IT AGAIN.

Crap, something else is coloured horribly! I do the compulsion for that and then it dawns on me that the class has actually moved on to something else. Everybody was writing something down from the board, so I look. Bad numbers.

Well, it is Business Studies!

Compulsion. Compulsion. Compulsion.

I try to down write the acceptable numbers down while holding my breath, but I can't get them PERFECT!

They are never neat enough! They smudge! I have to do them again. This time, I do it with my eyes closed and my breath held.

Of course I would make a mistake! That's the kind of useless idiot I am! I have to do it again!

I now have to perfect the numbers I messed up, but on the way down to the page, my pen nicks a bit of the paper and makes a tiny ink bubble. I draw a box around it, as if trying to contain a virus. Minuscule bits of ink stick out of the sides. It infuriates me. I want to scream. I have to keep drawing, drawing until the little black box of ink on the page has developed into a huge rectangle.

My teacher looks up, notices this and gives out to me. I'm told I'll be standing for the rest of the class if I don't pay attention, and I get a little scared. I'm angry anyway. I want to flip the desk (symmetrically) and run out of the classroom for being interrupted during my compulsion, but I don't, obviously.

Frustrated and sad, I clench my fists, duck my head quickly, do the compulsions and start crying like a baby. It's only to myself though. Nobody else noticed it … I hope. I guess my teacher was angrier than I thought because she kept me back after class to talk to me. I never got to know what it was about because as soon as I realised all the kids were gone out of the classroom, I burst out crying AGAIN.

I tried to stop myself. I wanted a calm, composed telling-off, where I would promise to listen and do better before running off to German. I would say, "Yes, Miss, I'm sorry and I will try to concentrate better." I would say sorry a thousand times and escape. But no, I decide to open my big mouth and start crying again.

My teacher wasn't mad though, to my surprise. She was actually very nice about it, telling me there's no hurry and I should dry my eyes, even though this was cutting into her Fifth Year's Maths time. It was then that I knew my OCD was bigger than I had thought. I could pretend all I liked, but it was now getting me into trouble. I used to pride myself on the fact that it wasn't affecting school and that they wouldn't find out about it.

Well, that just went out the window.

I had to go to the bathroom to dry my eyes, wondering how on Earth I could possibly go to German class after that. I stayed there. I didn't want to leave. What if somebody saw the red rims around my eyes? If they asked what the matter was, that would set me off again. All the other classes were in session as I trailed across the school to German, and had to sit through a video on World War Two. Surprisingly I didn't get in trouble for arriving late. My teacher's back was turned and I slipped in quietly. It was hard to concentrate, and not just because I'm not a war fanatic.

When I got home, I told Mom and she said, "Right. This has gone too far." She rang up the school immediately, telling the secretary she needs an appointment with our Principal. That, I am scared of. ULTRA SCARED.

Now I have to go to school tomorrow while, somewhere, people are talking about me.

Damn it. "Dammit, Janet. I love you!" (It's a song!)

✦

Forgetthedate/5/2013

Nothing much to report here. I should be watching a DVD but instead I'm watching Big Fat Gypsy Weddings. You would think the word 'petticoat' sounds dainty, yet this girl has so many layers she looks like a piece of cauliflower.

The teachers know about my thingymabob because the Principal had a staff meeting. My Mom and Dad went to him and discussed it. They said he noticed it before and thought about OCD before we had ever said anything, because I was walking in a weird way and my grades were slipping. They seem to want to help! I'm lucky!

It was a bit strange knowing that they knew something so personal about me. It's like, now, every time I will tap my nose in class, they'll know why. And it freaks me out.

Some of my friends know, and my cousins. They are really nice about it and, though they don't mention it often, they just seem to understand. It feels great to be able to talk about something as personal as that to them.

A couple of people saw me straightening things in my house and said, "You SO have OCD, Rebecca" as a joke.

I would pause and think, "Aw crap, they've hit the nail on the head and they don't even know it."

I'm not sure exactly how I told everyone I had it. I told my friends recently after they randomly posed it as a conversation topic.

"Have you ever heard of OCD?"

"Yup. I know ALL about THAT."

"Why, do you have it?"

"Mm-hm."

Then it was out. Boom!

✦

Today I went to the Educational Psychologist my doctor recommended. We went to her actual HOUSE, which has an office connected to it with all these diplomas and awards hanging on the wall. She has huge cube-shaped bookshelves with loads and loads of binders and files in them. The table is round with a bunch of pens scattered around. She is very nice! She's called Suzanne and she made me hot chocolate!

We sat down to have a chat about what was going to happen. "Okay," she said.

"Your parents can go away for an hour or so while I test you and when they come back, we'll give you the results." My first reaction was, "What? You're leaving me with a strange lady?" I didn't even know why I was at this person's house in the first place. Nevertheless, my parents went off shopping and I started the test.

I was very shy, really. I was playing with my hands while she was talking to me.

For the IQ test, we started off with little green blocks. I was shown a picture and had to make the blocks look like it, by arranging them on a board marked with guidelines. I thought, "Sheesh, a baby could do that".

BOY WAS I WRONG.

It was easy the first few times, but then the guideline board was removed and I couldn't tell AT ALL what I was making. Then she added more blocks and asked me to copy a more complex picture.

She also asked me to repeat series of numbers forwards and backwards, to test my memory. I was able to do it for the most part, until she started calling out bad numbers. I asked if she could substitute them and she began asking why. I was thinking, "You know why! You know very well! My doctor referred me to you!", but I kept up the pretence and told her it was because of my OCD and could she pretty, pretty please substitute the numbers? She said she would, and it went smoothly from there.

She asked stuff I perceived as pointless such as, "Why do policemen wear uniforms?" and I was actually stumped. I'd never thought about it before. I guess it was to test ... I don't know, my social maturity? I'm not even going to speculate, because I'll end up sounding ridiculous.

I had to look at a row of pictures and make associations between them such as, "Toothbrush is like sock because when you get up in the morning, you come into contact with both of those items while getting ready for school." I had to spell things. I had to read out a passage and got mad in my head when I couldn't pronounce some words because I DID KNOW THEM!

We had a break and she made me a BEAUTIFUL hot chocolate with about 3cm of foam. YUMMY.

Then my parents came back and we had a discussion.

It turns out my literacy is extremely good (95/99) and I'm in the top 2% in the country for English. She said my IQ was above average.

Suzanne also said that I need to get out more. She said it nicer than that though. On my report it said my "social interactions seemed developmentally immature." I've always known I was a six year-old in a thirteen year-old's body!

I don't really know what to think right now. I'm not exactly sure why I even went to her today. I'm not really sure what I'm doing anymore. My parents took away my laptop today. I thought I was in trouble when I saw it was gone. I asked, "What did I do wrong?" And they said, "Nothing. You just need to stop using it for now. It doesn't help."

So then, it was gone. I was still confused as to why it had gone, and I was mad at my parents because I thought they were purposely trying to take away the one thing that didn't trigger my OCD as much. It took me a while to realise they were doing me a favour.

After a visit to Sylvia's house the next day, I got a little surprise. When

I returned home, I was handed this little bottle. It was white and said 5-HTP which I found out stood for Hydroxy Tryptophan, whatever that is. It was basically a herbal pill instead of real medication. My parents said they wanted to try herbal remedies before the last resort of medication. They said it would help me. I wasn't exactly pleased, but they were trying so hard, I didn't want to say no.

"I'm supposed to be reassured because it comes from a plant? COCAINE comes from a plant and where did that get us?"

That one made them laugh.

+

My OCD was getting worse all the time. I could do very little to prevent it from worsening. It got to the point where I could barely hold a conversation. My friends noticed it more and more, and I was worried they were beginning to think of me as some freak of nature.

Our lunch breaks would consist of them perhaps asking me a question but only finally getting the answer thirty to forty seconds later. They'd go, "What?" because by then the conversation had changed. I was only answering to keep up the impression that I was actually not an arrogant kid who didn't give a damn about what they were saying.

I had to keep stopping when I would walk around the school because if I didn't walk in the 'right' routes it would act like a ginormous itch that I had to scratch.

I would be relieved when it was class time, but that would dissolve as soon as I sat down because then I'd have to sit through forty minutes of triggers. My school days consisted of internalised arguments, no learning whatsoever. There's this great chunk I missed out on in class. Even my writing was affected, because I had to count everything. It sucked.

I could never just go home at the end of school. I had to shield my eyes from all the asymmetrical items around me and, if I didn't, I'd have to make them symmetrical.

I hated my house and school and I felt I was making everyone around me sad.

✦

One day at school, I heard laughter while I was zoning out over a book during study time. At first I thought they were laughing at some joke or other, but when I turned around, I saw it was directed at me. They had started noticing my compulsions. When they started pointing at each other and tapping their noses while looking at me, I wanted to explode. They must have seen me doing it while I was trying to study.

Wherever I went in the school, I'd see one of their friends, calling me, getting me to look at them tapping their noses. I'll never forget their delighted little faces.

The bell rang for break. My friend asked me why I was shaking. I regret not shouting out, screaming or throwing something at them. Don't worry, I'm not violent. I'd only kill them a little bit.

It was infuriating. They'd stop me in the halls just to tap their noses at me. I know to them it must have looked funny and I can understand that, but it wasn't exactly helpful. Now, the majority of my Year did NOT do this, and were extremely nice. I was (and still am) extremely lucky to be in a Year with lovely people. There was only a small percentage who made fun of me. Even then, it wasn't too bad. I can see why they found it funny, and so it didn't bother me too much.

At the start of the next school year, I talked to our school chaplain to get the matter resolved, as they didn't forget it throughout the summer and it extended into Second Year. Some of them even apologised, which was great. It was only light teasing, and I certainly don't mean to dig up old news, dead and buried, but this is my book and I want to report everything to do with OCD. This is real life.

When the school year was nearly over, and classes had started to wind down, desks were moved into the cafeteria hall for our First Year exams. We carried the desks there ourselves but I nearly dropped mine down the stairs. It was a long way to the cafeteria, the only room big enough to hold all of us. We had been preparing all year for this, but now we began to study, day and night, even in class time.

My classmates' heads would be down, but mine would be swivelling around, constantly picking up on triggers. No classroom was free of triggers. Something blue or something to do with 4 was in every room. Bad words were always spoken, seen, or read. It was hard to study.

When it came to the first exam day, we were given our timetables, our allocated seats in the cafeteria and told we had an hour to study before each subject.

   We sat in rows, by class and in alphabetical order. I was sitting beside people I knew well. Some of them spent the time messing or chatting, Others actually put their heads down and studied. I badly wanted to study. I wanted to be able to put my head down and soak up the information like a sponge. I wanted the opportunity to feel that confidence rush, the feeling you get when you know you're going to pass. I had the opportunity, but I couldn't take it.

   The first test was CSPE. If you don't know what that is, it's where you learn about the laws of a country, the parliament and taking care of the Earth. I spent the pre-test hour trying to study. Then the papers were handed out and, after a few nervous glances and excited shuffling, the whole cafeteria fell into complete silence.

We had to tick boxes, write explanations, describe things and answer true or false. Just your basic end-of-year test, really. The usual.

When we were finished, we handed up the sheets and began studying for the next test. Switching to something completely different from the last subject was a little difficult. I kept thinking about the previous one, but it was okay after a while. After that test concluded, we went home.

That was the general routine for the end-of-year tests. It wasn't easy for anyone. It's hard to completely focus on a topic you might not really care about. It's even harder to develop enough interest necessary to pass when the subject seems utterly pointless. It's just something that needs to be done.

It was extremely hard for me to study, both at home and at school. I would read a page of History, see a 'bad' word, number or colour and start tapping my nose to blow the bad luck away. Sometimes, I would be so frustrated that I would just slam the book down or throw my pencil across the room or something. I'd then feel my way into the sitting room and flop down on the couch. Not constructive, I know, but it was predictable.

The tests continued. I was really only there to register myself in roll call. There was so little that I had absorbed during the year. All the other kids were doing so well. I heard them talk, going over their answers with each other, and I realised they weren't anything like mine. I heard certain answers that sparked something in my mind, memories of things I might vaguely have heard. I immediately knew they were correct and cringed at the fact I could have got it right if I had somehow recalled them, and willed my hand to write them down.

All these thoughts were filling time where I should be have been recovering and relaxing. I should have been slumped on a wall with my friends, airing mindless topics of conversation, but I was far too busy with thoughts, compulsions and rituals.

Anyway, on the last day, we finished up our tests and said goodbye to each other. It was very odd leaving school. My friends and I were making plans to hang out afterwards, but when I got to the car, I found my therapist had brought the appointment date forward to that day at five, so I couldn't join them. I got to bring home leftover crisps from the school shop, though. Everything was out of routine and it felt extremely odd. I had to say goodbye to all my friends (well, three of them) and head home to do … something.

What was I supposed to do?

Entertain me. Tap your nose.

Chapter Eight
Summertime

Summer is the best time of the year for many people, especially teenagers. They like to go to the beach with their friends or hang out, making the most of the (hopefully) good weather. Personally, I prefer winter, but that's only because there's an excuse to stay in and play Zelda all day.

I love snow and I love the cold. It's way more fun than sticky, unpredictable summer. It's unpredictable because good weather disrupts routine. In winter, activity options are limited, therefore every day is more or less predictable. In summer, people might go to the beach one day and to a friend's barbecue the next.

My parents enjoy social activities throughout the year, but especially, unfortunately for me, in summertime. I get nervous if we visit someone else's house, because I don't know what's going to happen, where we will sit, what we will eat and so on.

Unlike most teenagers, I can't say that it was a relief to relax and be off school for summer holidays – it wasn't. I couldn't work much during class anyway.

Summer was an inconvenience. My compulsions worsened significantly, and soon my best buddy, OCD, was with me every moment of the day and night. I became less resistant to it, because summer is an idle time. It meant there was less of a chance of me becoming occupied with something to take away from my obsessions. So I occupied myself by exploring a special area of interest: Sleep Study (you'll find more about that later).

Despite the season, so far every day was the same. That was good. Some days Mom and I might go into town to shop, or we would just sit and chat. We would wait for Dad to come home so I could go out and play with him and Shadow, my dog. Everything was routine and I liked it like that.

I took my herbal pill thing every day. It tasted like grass (not that I've eaten it), and a handful of cod liver oil drops. Mom said they will help my brain. I went to CBT whenever I had to. I make it sound like a huge inconvenience, don't I? I honestly don't mean it like that. It's just I was afraid of doing anything. Very afraid.

Meanwhile, my parents were looking around for summer camps that I could do. They said it would keep me busy. I saw THAT as an inconvenience, and worried about how I was supposed to interact with other summer campers when my OCD kept bugging me. They were there all the time. There were so many ins and outs to the compulsions, I couldn't keep up. It was like having an unnecessarily thorough airport Customs search every single day. It got to the point where I had to judge whether or not it would be worth it to go to the bathroom, or to mount an expedition to the kitchen to get something to eat or drink.

This is the kind of conversation I'd have in my head for every action every day:

"I have to go to the bathroom."

Really? You have to?

"Yeah!"

Okay, you brought this upon yourself. You know the drill. Close your eyes. You don't want to see any triggers, do you?

"They're closed."

Yeah, but that was a test. You may have seen a wood knot without realising it. You may have also seen something blue. You never know.

"Yes I do."

Do you really? I'm on your side. I'm trying to save you from cancer and sadness here! Quit being stubborn and do what I say!

"You aren't on my side. You are me. You're OCD and you're not logical."

Tap your nose and blow it away. Make sure not to point it towards your parents. You don't want to infect them with cancer and sadness do you?

"Are you serious?! That won't work!"

How could you possibly know? Tap your nose and blow the possible blue and wood knots away, before you come into contact with more.

"Fine."

Somebody says 'blue' in the middle of my compulsion

Blue! Do your compulsion again! Restart it! In fact, do it twice! Just to be on the safe side! Don't open your eyes!

Compulsion

Did you point it away from your parents?

"Of course!"

Sweetie, that wasn't an actual question. That was a polite way of making you do it again.

"Look, I KNOW I did it right."

HOW do you know?! Are you really selfish enough to leave it like this? You could have just given cancer to your parents and you're thinking of leaving? DO. IT. AGAIN.

Compulsion

Good girl. Now keep your eyes shut. Did you open them? No? Okay, I'll let it slide. There isn't enough evidence to support my claim. Now get up and feel your way to the door.

"Okay."

You didn't step on the correct part of the floor, you idiot! And you almost had it! Go back!

"But my eyes are closed! I can't tell where the spot was!"

It was just back there, trust me!

CUE WEIRD STEPPING ON FLOOR

Are you sure that was it?

"I'M SURE!"

Okay then. Now go to the door. Do not open your eyes. Do your ritual for the door. You know, six taps of the feet for each side of the door frame, which makes thirty-six taps, and then do twelve more since it's a set of double doors.

Compulsion

"Finished."

You can do better than that. This is a game for you, isn't it?

"No!"

Then take this seriously. Do it again.

Compulsion

Now, you go out the door, across the hall, and STEP WHERE I TELL YOU TO STEP. You'll know by the feeling of the floor. I'm the boss here.

"Since when did you become the boss of me?!"

Go back. It was inevitable. Go back to the door. Step around the area that you know was wrong. Tap and slide your foot on the floor until I tell you to stop.

"If it makes you shut up."

Good. Now take hold of the banisters and go upstairs. Do not open your eyes for one second, even when you get to the top.

YOU DIDN'T TOUCH THE BANISTER RIGHT! Go halfway down the stairs, backwards, and do it again!

Compulsion

Now, you're at the archway. Do it, tap your feet for the special archway ritual.

Compulsion

A narrow escape, well done. Now do your doorway ritual for the bathroom.

Compulsion

You did not do it correctly. You got cocky after the archway ritual, thinking you could get it all right. I'll soon have that knocked out of you. Do it again!

Compulsion

Are you serious? WRONG! AGAIN!

Compulsion

You're just playing, aren't you? Seriously, I'd hurry up if I were you. You don't want to stay here all day do you?

Compulsion

Why can't you get it right?

"I DON'T KNOW!"

"Rebecca, where are you?" shouts my Mom from downstairs.

She could have been talking about the number 4 to someone before she shouted. 4 means death. Tap your nose.

"In a minute."

Tap it NOW!

"Rebecca, why aren't you answering me?"

"She wasn't talking about 4."

She was, she was. Naïve little fool. YOU THOUGHT ABOUT 4!

Tap your nose.

*Compul---

"REBECCA!"

"WHAT?!"

Why did you stop? Why? You almost had it, if that stupid mother of yours wouldn't shut her gob! Oh, how bad you are for thinking something like that! That's bad luck! Another compulsion added to your queue!

"I-I'm just doing a habit, Mom!"

"Okay. Don't be too long."

Okay, now start again. If you don't, I'll blame the interruption on your mother and she will die.

"That won't happen."

Just how can you possibly know?

✦

As the summer wore on, things looked up a little. My cousin came over and for once, we actually had nice weather. It was gorgeous. We set up a basketball net in the yard and started having competitions. Every morning we went to an art camp run by Ms Doherty. My cousin and I had our own table at the back of the room, where we could mess around as much as we liked … unless she was watching.

We got to make our own animations, using her flashy Mac with Final Cut Pro and Photoshop on it. I felt like a professional. Amazingly, that fabulous Mac was just casually sitting there in the back of our art room. If I had one like that, I'd be sticking signposts on the wall so visitors could come and BEHOLD it the minute they stepped in.

It was extremely hot that summer. We aren't used to that in Ireland, so the camp's break-times consisted mainly of everyone huddling under a sun umbrella sticking out of a picnic table. It was funny. Ms Doherty's house is really nice and her daughter has blue and purple hair. So yeah, our animation is up on YouTube. I'm embarrassed by it now, but it was a hard process, so NO JUDGING! I never realised animators worked so hard. I categorised animation as having the same level of difficulty as playing a video game, but it is really amazing what those people can do.

My other cousin came back from a holiday in Portugal and she came and hung out with us. It was such fun, even though I had to be given twenty minutes in advance to get up the stairs at bedtime. A great portion of my holiday was, surprisingly, now being spent having fun. Actually, looking back on it now, my 2013 summer was excellent in terms of activities.

My parents and I realised that OCD didn't hinder my life so much if it didn't have any idleness to feed on, so we made sure I had plenty to do.

✦

"Go on, Rebecca. You can do it!"

Once again, I am at the kitchen table. Mr Collins has suggested keeping a diary about OCD, so I have a notebook with a flowery design in front of me and a pen beside it. The flowery design is composed of purple and lilac shaded flowers with a purple/wine-coloured spiral spine. I have to make an entry. But not every entry can be the same. I have to do more ERP. My Dad is strolling around the kitchen, dropping teabags into mugs like a professional. My Mom is hovering behind me, which I normally don't mind, but this time it's not very fun. I have a remote control sitting on the table beside the notebook. I have to move it.

What a challenge (!).

Yes, that was complete sarcasm. It's something a two year-old can do, so I should be able to. I continue to refuse my parents, saying I have things to do, privately knowing all I have to do is more compulsions.

But they make me do it.

I just stared at the remote. My parents and I had fought about this all morning. It was like that one dreaded chore that you knew you had to do sometime, but chose to put it off for as long as you could. I hated them for forcing me. My parents were one step away from grabbing my hand and moving it for me. I wished they had. But they wouldn't. They couldn't do it for me. Besides, they had other things to do. So did I.

I grabbed the remote and turned it sideways. It lasted three seconds before I caved in and straightened it.

It's like everything went out of kilter for those three seconds. The whole world stopped. The kettle stopped boiling, people on TV stopped speaking, people froze in the streets and time had given up. The colour drained from everything. Everything was wrong in those three seconds.

I found myself staring at the straightened remote control again. Surely I could have done better than that. To heck with the self-pitying mental descriptions of what it felt like. I know I could have done better.

"Can you do it again?" Mom said. I looked at her angrily and said, "No." It was over for today.

"Write it down, so."

I picked up the pen and opened the notebook, while Dad strolled over to the kitchen table and sat down. I leaned over my book and chewed my pen thoughtfully.

"It was only three seconds. It was crap. I did CRAP. What am I supposed to write if I didn't do anything?!"

"How about," Dad said, setting up his laptop, "'I moved the remote control for three seconds, and I am proud.'"

I wasn't proud, but I wrote it down nevertheless.

I had finished my homework.

Chapter Nine

Activities and Inspirations

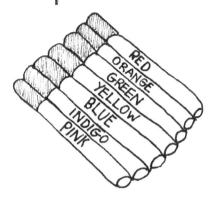

Towards the end of that summer, I went to Galway with my friend Sylvia. We left at eleven in the morning, to get the maximum experience. We were telling ghost stories on the way up, which I find I always regret at night. We went on the big motorway.

Sylvia was very nice about the OCD thing, especially as we walked around the city. She told me where the squares in the street got bigger and smaller so I could be prepared. She told me whether the street was clear to cross or whether there was a group of people coming in my direction. Sylvia and her family were so understanding. In their house, they didn't mind if I straightened their things. They would sometimes straighten everything even before I got there. I can't thank them enough. They never asked any questions. Not many would keep inviting a person with such severe OCD and helping them along like that.

We went into a bookshop and browsed. I could have stayed all day in the stationery section. I like the smell of these places, and their structured prices and chainstore products. I like the signs that say 50% off , and enjoy working out prices in my head to calculate the money I need. I don't always get it right, but it's fun to try. I like the brightly-coloured pens and the convenient office storage boxes. I like looking inside the books and at the blurbs on the back to see what the story is about. I love bookshops.

We carried on walking and found Kennedy Park. We got ice creams and sat down on benches, looking at the stuff we bought. Then we went into a Japanese restaurant. I had pale brown flat noodles with chicken on the top. I ordered a Coke, but drank it all before my food got to the table, because that is what I do when the dinner takes too long to arrive. I chucked the complimentary lemon to the side of my plate. I liked lemons when I was younger, but now, not so much.

My day in Galway was a lot of fun, thanks to Sylvia and her family. I went home happy that day.

The end of summer wasn't all roses though. You're probably thinking, "OH GREAT! Here she goes again!" I can understand that, but I'm not going to miss out on important events. Roses have thorns.

Besides enjoying some happy rainbows, I was still living through a strictly-prioritised pattern of actions. The severity of my obsessions and compulsions was linked to my moods.

I would became obsessed with a particular topic. Every so often, maybe once or twice a year, I latch onto a subject and become so obsessed with it, that it's all I think and talk about. If something sparks inspiration, I could be on an 'Inspiration High' a.k.a. Topic Obsession for ages.

My obsessive interest of summer 2013 was Sleep Study. Yes, I know, it's a weird topic. You might not even know what it is. I studied things like the science behind sleep, REM sleep, paralysis and dreams. I have no idea why I became obsessed, but I have a small collection books on the topic and a long internet history of sleep-related Google searches.

Two years ago, I got obsessed with ventriloquism: the skill of talking through a dummy or puppet. Yup, the ventriloquist puts their hand where the sun doesn't shine and moves the puppet's mouth, while trying to talk without moving their own mouth, so it looks like the puppet is speaking. What sparked my obsession with ventriloquism was a clip on the internet that my Dad's workmate told him to look up. It was of a guy named Jeff Dunham who had dummies named Achmed and Peanut. I loved the shows.

I somehow wangled a nice Idiot's Guide to Ventriloquism from an online store. Sylvia also found an Edgar Bergen (celebrity ventriloquist) guide on how to become one. I bought three puppets and practised with them.

Then that obsession played itself out, and I moved on to something else. I might have none for a while and then I'd get another spike of inspiration. It's awesome.

If somebody talked to me, the only thing I would talk about was my latest obsession. I'm sure some people got bored, but I was so enthralled that I didn't care. Coupling that with my OCD, you could say my whole summer was filled with obsessions, some welcome and some resented. Sleep study was a brilliant thing to turn to. Other things weren't as welcome.

The herbal serotonin remedy wasn't working for me, so we decided we had to roll in the big guns and take real meds!

Well, that was hell.

You have to allow a certain period of time to pass for a medicine, herbal or otherwise, to leave your system, or the new medicines might interact. So, I waited for the necessary period, and my doctor wrote me a prescription. I'd given into pharmaceuticals. I wasn't proud, but I was willing to try anything.

The inbetween time I spent on NO medicine of any kind was like an OCD rebound. Every minute of every day was consumed. I couldn't do anything. It was horrible for my parents, not to mention my friends! Even so, I would still be invited over, with my friends and family straightening everything before my visit. I was very grateful for that, but I was still going to check!

I would notice a lot of details, so I could spot triggers all around me. A girls'-day-out with Mom turned into a row about my walking-on-lines thing, which then became a textbook mother-and-daughter thing, not an adventure. Everyone was trying to make it work, but you shouldn't have to try. You should be able to enjoy everyday life, without it being a trying task.

This rebound spike, I guess you could call it, was so bad that, once, I was up until three in the morning trying to get through the arch leading to my bedroom. I couldn't do it, after trying over and over again, and had to sleep with my parents. I needed to go to the bathroom after standing out there for three hours, but my parent's walk-in wardrobe/bathroom also had an arch leading to it, so, to avoid dealing with that, we had to trail downstairs in the dark. Mom's hands were around me as I closed my eyes. She led me to the kitchen and stopped when I had to do my rituals. She didn't say anything when I did the same ones over again because I didn't get them right. She warned me when we came to the tiles in the kitchen. I opened my eyes a crack and cupped my hands around my eyes like binoculars, so I would pick up on any potential triggers in my peripheral vision. I could see just enough to make out the lines between the tiles.

I wouldn't even get dressed without my little mind-buddy telling me to do something else. At one point I just lay on the floor and read a book. I didn't want to get dressed. I yanked a load of clothes out of my wardrobe one morning because I was so frustrated.

Finally I was able to start taking the new meds, but they kicked in so gradually that I often wondered whether I was taking real medication or a sugar pill, because every day seemed the same. Grey. Monotonous. Maybe it was a placebo, I wondered.

Because you have to wait for it to build up in your system, I didn't notice exactly when things started to get better. But things did get better. By that, I mean my head stopped swirling around so much. I could actually think straight for once. And it felt awesome. I wasn't worrying quite so continuously, though I still held tight to my habits. The medication began to allow me to do things I couldn't have done before.

I started CBT again. I wasn't sure how it was going to go, because the last sessions didn't really work. However, I now had the backup of medication, and this time I was more optimistic. My therapist, my parents and I discussed how my OCD thoughts worked. I wrote descriptions of each obsession, although, with the amount I had, I was reluctant to describe them all.

We talked about how the obsessions made me feel, the impact they had on school and social life, and weighed the negatives against the positives. The positives of having OCD are that you are very cautious and detail-orientated, among other things.

Stupid as it may seem, I felt almost sorry for OCD, we were trashing it so much. I had become protective of my own. After all, I had it my whole life, ever since I was born. I firmly believe that, all the way back to when I was four, giving my mom the toy every day, OCD felt like a cuddle blanket, in my mind. It was like a best friend. I didn't want it to go. I had always cuddled the same metaphorical blanket, even when I was small. The prospect of dumping it was terrifying. I had never lived without it. But I had to take my mind off that somehow, and let the process … well … be processed.

Life had to get in the way.

✦

Looking back at the summer of 2013, it had been filled with fun activities, with little time to be bored.

I had stayed up in my cousin's house and it was hilarious. I was usually afraid to stay anywhere but my own house, but I had a great time! We went to the beach every day and screamed in shock at the coldness of the water. We made YouTube videos and got a load of American candy from the local store and did taste tests. There's this thing called Marshmallow Fluff that is basically just a big tub of marshmallow paste. It is the most delicious thing ever. I want to go to America!

We laughed all the time and it was great. Even though I still had to get up during the night to straighten everything, it was really fun. I'm looking forward to doing it again.

Subsequently, I also disclosed my OCD to that cousin and to my cousin Róisín as well, so when Róisín came with us on holiday to Kerry, she understood why I straightened everything. She was only ten, but she was amazing. She let me hang onto her shoulder when we had to cross the tiny hexagonal squares in the hotel lobby and told me where the squares got smaller and bigger, and where I'd have to jump. We went to Easons together and I got a Manga magazine. We had bunk beds to sleep in and would rotate from top to bottom bunk each night. It was like a mini apartment, and Róisín and I could go down to the Kid's Club for video games, popcorn and Mean Girls any time we wanted.

We ate a mountain of bread rolls at dinner time. It was crazy. She was hilarious too. Every time I said something bad about One Direction, she shouted "BLUE, BLUE, BLUE!" which made us all laugh. It was especially funny when I had to do exactly what she intended to make me do, the compulsion. I laughed too. I couldn't help it. Credit to Róisín for being sneaky. Well, at least I hit her with my slap watch. That made it all better.

She hit me back, though.

Chapter Ten
The Start of a New School Year

On the 28th of August 2013, I'm standing outside secondary school once again. I was so hyper last night, I couldn't sleep. The prospect of coming back to a routine place where I'd be with kids my own age all day is really exciting.

I am in Second Year now. I am no longer one of the babies of the school. This is a whole new generation, and one of my best friends, Sylvia, is a part of it. She's joining First Year this year and it's great. It's been ages since I went to school with her.

Well, a year.

Everybody is standing outside the school, chatting and hugging each other. I walk awkwardly up to my friends and say, "Hi." Yes, I'm quite the socialite.

My friends go to hug me and I squeeze my body stiff and accept it. I'm not the best at hugging, or what they call 'banter'. I'm glad to see my friends. They're the people that got me used to this place, with all its weird little deviances from primary school.

Everybody is catching up on what had happened over the summer. I interject, telling them I went to Kerry. I show them this funny little satchel that I got in Killarney with Róisín. It's really cute.

After a while, we are brought inside. I choose my steps carefully on the tiled stone floor. Welcome back to the blue world of school. The nice, communal colour of education. That, or green. If only it were green.

I don't get to say 'Hi' to Sylvia, as the First Years start school before the other years. We are led into the cafeteria to listen to a speech from the Principal.

"Second Year is the most important year in secondary school. It's the time where you decide whether you are going to work with, or against the system. Although all the years are important, Second Year is the most important year in this school."

It always feels really serious when the Principal talks to us – he sounds so strict, even though he's probably very nice. I suppose you have to be strict when you're in charge of five hundred adolescents.

We are led upstairs into a room and divided up into our respective classes. My classroom is down at the end of the corridor. We are brought in and given timetables – I wince at the numbers, and begin my compulsion. It's a good thing I'm in the front desk so people can't see me. We are given our new journals. They are red this year. I couldn't really look at my journal last year, as it was dark blue, so red is perfect, and it has nice gold writing on the front.

I have the luxury of having a greeny-blue locker this year, a step above the royal BLUE locker last year. We also find out who is our Year Head.

We only have a half day today, so we quickly get to go home. Nevertheless, the summer feeling has well and truly gone. I wonder how Sylvia did on the first day. I'm really excited for her to meet my friends so we can go around in a big group.

September, 2013

The people at school seem to have forgotten about the nose-tapping business from last year. That's good. I got a locker near my friends, which is also very convenient. We are mushed in with the Third Years in the locker area, and there's ninety of us Second Years alone, so break times when we get our books can be crazy. We are frequently up against each other's butts trying to get to the next class.

The locker area is tiled, so I have to be extremely careful when navigating it. A bunch of kids can throw you off balance, and I end up tripping over my own feet a lot. The good thing is, the squares are quite big and easy to walk on if you concentrate. I'm generally good at it. It's like stepping on Hollywood Walk of Fame stars compared to the miniscule bricks in the Killarney hotel.

Seriously, floor cracks are EVERYWHERE!

It was odd being in a new year at the start, but, a month into it, everybody seems to be settling down. My friends have befriended each other and we hang out every day. The new students seem to fit in well.

There's this huge chunk of learning I'm missing from First Year classes that I have to make up for in Second Year, so I'm going to concentrate on that, while learning all the new stuff.

It's going to be challenging, but I'm going to try my best.

As the months went by, my OCD behaved itself, like a little puppy. I was working around it to achieve at least partly acceptable grades. I was convinced the medicine was working. It turns out you can't get too cocky.

Things started changing again. My compulsions became worse and I couldn't pay attention in class anymore.

My first reaction to this was, "Oh, God, it's happening again." It never really went away, but it hadn't asserted itself in a long while. Perhaps due to the medication. Now, though, I couldn't tolerate the number 2. I hated it, because two by two is four, and you all know where I'm going with that one. I could write it, but not speak or hear it. That was three numbers I couldn't use. Also, I started to split up numbers. For instance, if I had to write '12', I'd put a huge line between the 1 and 2, so the devious multiple of 4 couldn't be reached. It made sure the numbers reverted back to their original form, and not anything to do with evil numbers.

I also started to split up words. Before, I used to have to add on extra words, to avoid the '4' multiple, but I found a cheat. Some words could be split up into logical words (or at least they were logical to me) to reach the desired amount in a sentence.

For instance, if I had to write 'market' in an essay, I'd put a line through it, so 'mark' and 'et' were separate. These are logical words because Mark is a name, and E.T. is the name of the alien in the Spielberg film. So, it makes two words.

If I did write 'market', I might also start thinking about market stalls selling fresh fruit and vegetables. That would morph into an image of an evil man wielding a butcher's knife, selling dismantled components of my family's bodies to the crowd. I couldn't ask for help, because everybody would be evil. Even the uniformed guards, whom I find extremely safe and comforting in the face of adversity, would turn on me. There would be blood everywhere and his bloody mouth would open saying, "You're next, but you know how to stop this, don't you? Tap your nose. Blow it away, you selfish idiot."

"And that's why Jesus was crucified."

I snap my head up, disorientated. Where am I again? Oh yeah, Religion class. The class that can be great fun sometimes and numbingly tedious at other times (no offence, Miss). It's coming back to me. I can remember coming through the door and sitting down thirty minutes ago. I would have got the compulsion correct in a shorter amount of time, but with everybody talking around me and constant triggers flying back and forth, it took me a longer time to concentrate. Plus, I think some people are laughing.

I turn around.

Yup, people are looking me dead in the eye, tapping their noses. Damn it. It's started again. The tapping and the smiling – not enough to constitute bullying, but definitely enough to make me feel extremely uncomfortable. I am angry. I managed to get past one month of school without anybody reacting to my compulsions, and now this. My mind swarms with metaphorical bees, buzzing "WILL YOU JUST LEARN YOUR RELIGION FOR CHRIST'S SAKE?!"

I turn around and stick my middle finger straight up at the kids across the room. They nearly burst out laughing. Goal reached. Rebecca noticed, ten points to Gryffindor.

I turn back and slump into the chair. I pretend to study the fabulous whitewash brickwork of our school walls only to be tapped on the shoulder by the kid sitting behind me. I turn around.

"They're laughing at you, Rebecca. Look at them."

"Like I care."

"Why do you do that, though?"

"I just do."

"Does this person have some sympathy with me?" I ponder, but my worst fear is quickly confirmed as I realise she is laughing along just as merrily with the others, who are still tapping their noses.

"Damn you and all your idiot friends", I whisper, before looking to the teacher for a clue as to where we are in our syllabus.

OCD has been described as many things, even as some kind of voodoo.

Yes, fear me, peers. I will seal your windpipes with one touch of a finger against my magical facial cartilage.

I wish.

✦

But it doesn't matter now. The bell rings

Religion is over, and I grab my bag and bang my way out the door. It's extremely helpful in these situations to be the kid closest to the door – you can make quick exits. Not that I've needed to before this.

On my way to lunch, I can feel that I'm being watched as I make my way to the locker area. I rub my face with my fist for comfort. It actually works. It's something I do when I get nervous. I dump my books in double-quick time, slam the locker seven times (six is also a bad number now) and get my Kinder Bueno bar and Capri Sun (I have those every single day, and hot buttered rolls for small lunch).

I then hang out with my friends, in as much as I can. I know they think I'm dumb or crazy. Those are my own words, but you sure as hell can bet that's what they think. They are incredibly nice, but I know they are wondering what the heck planet I'm from.

The self-consciousness becomes almost natural as the weeks pass. I have an apprehensive feeling every time I enter the locker area. Once, I caught a group looking at my crack-avoiding and they were laughing, imitating my prancing walk. I slammed my locker and tried to make a dramatic exit. I flounced about two metres until I realized I needed to go back to the locker. The shutting of the door hadn't felt right. Besides, I had forgotten to put my coat in it. I slammed the locker door over and over again until it was just right, and ran off. I know I would have been longer if the school bell wasn't hurrying me.

I'm once again the kid who won't step on cracks.

I've been shouted at and laughed at for avoiding on them. I've been introduced as 'the girl who can't walk on cracks'. I've been goaded to step on a crack just to generate a laugh. I promptly told that person to watch their back (it was the only comeback I had at the time), which earned me a brand new peal of laughter.

It wasn't really bullying, more like teasing. It was a simple thin layer of dismal pressure surrounding my school life which would erupt during those brief encounters.

I understand why they thought it was funny. Even so, I'd like to think I wouldn't have behaved in the same way.

✦

It all got cleared up, though.

I was called out of class one day to talk to the school chaplain. I would never get called out of class, so this was a surprise. She brought me to her small room which had fluffy purple seats and various religious icons. She told me she had heard 'from a source' that I was feeling uncomfortable at school. I asked who this source was. She told me it was somebody in my year.

"Somebody in my year?" I thought. "Who in my year would do that?" Whoever did that I am really thankful and grateful to them. That was one really nice person.

I told the chaplain in detail about what was going on and, after a while, she finally got the truth out of me as to why I had these mannerisms. I tried to avoid the OCD label as much as I could, hoping possibly she could put me down as just one of the 'weird kids' who had eccentricities 'just because.' But, the more I avoided the dreaded acronym, the more insistently she pressed the issue.

So I told her.

"I have OCD. So ... yeah. There's that – and that's why I can't really concentrate in class. My grades have dropped and, things are … obsessive."

"Oh."

And, believe it or not, she wasn't surprised. She acted as if ten people walked into her office every day and declared this diagnosis. She knew what OCD was. I didn't have to explain myself. That was refreshing. We talked about it, and she asked me to hang in there. She assured me I wasn't alone and gave me ideas about tackling compulsions. I felt so grateful. Any opportunity to talk helps.

So, the issue got sorted out. Some of the kids even apologised, which was very nice of them.

The first time that happened, I was leaving Business Studies and two kids came up and said sorry. One of them had said sorry previously, which was very big of him. He wasn't involved very much at all anyway, but it was still nice of him. When I was called back twice to hear separate 'sorrys', I was so happy, I just cried. I cried like a baby getting my homework out of my locker. I was just really happy. All that discomfort hadn't lasted that long. Now, there would be plenty to worry about at school, but that was one thing off my mind. They all understood. Well, to a certain degree. Some more than others. Life was getting better.

✦

Things began to look up. They do say you feel worse before you feel better, which can be true. My family and friends were also being extremely nice and supportive about OCD, which was lovely of them. I continued to go to school. I never had to be interrupted by the compulsions enough to not go to school after that. I still had to close my eyes and feel my way around the house, but even so, things were getting better.

I noticed that my mood had improved in class. I wasn't too hyper. I could catch myself out when I felt my attention slipping, and focus my concentration back to the teacher. I no longer got half as frustrated as I had done previously. It was easier to get the compulsions done.

I began to listen in class and found I understood more than I had previously thought. I could grasp the idea of certain maths concepts. I could get them right. I couldn't write many of them, but the problems I could write, I had a better understanding of. I was put into Higher Level English and Irish, and Ordinary Level Maths. I was proud of that. It proved I could get better. I was capable of doing Ordinary Level, maybe I could even aim for Higher Level, if I wanted to be presumptuous.

I felt this exhilaration when I worked out something in my head and found I got it right on the board. It made me feel like Einstein, just for solving a simple equation. I felt happy! On a good day, I may only have to do compulsions two or three times each, as opposed to the ten or twelve repetitive behaviours per compulsion I'm used to. That was a godsend.

To be fair, I did have bad days. I did have days where I couldn't go anywhere or do anything without getting angry or scared or both. Those days felt like setbacks, but I began to believe that there would be other days where I could have almost all of the freedom I wanted. I could do my homework and concentrate on it. I could actually take in what I was learning. And that made me want to scream with joy.

With periodic CBT appointments, I continued to improve. Challenging your thoughts every once in a while is good. CBT was just a definite set period for thought-analysing. It was brilliant. My mind was altering. I wasn't stopping my compulsions, but something was happening in my brain. I didn't think I'd ever want to get rid of OCD, but, here I was, persevering with the process, doing the CBT. It was gradual, not sudden, so I kind of took it for granted. I slowly began to feel like I could take more on board and went with it. I was starting to get happier and think clearer. It was creepily awesome.

I was still very scared of leaving OCD – my cuddle blanket. Life would be radically different without compulsions. How could I live without them? I hated them, but they were my family too.

September and October of 2013 was the best time of my life. I would never have admitted I needed OCD if I hadn't taken the medication. When I'd started taking it, it felt like I was getting worse, (you don't hear many people saying that), but it turns out it was just another phase in recovery.

Yes, I can call it that. Recovery. I can finally call it that. It's never straightforward. But I'm glad it's that way.

✦

September, 2013

First, I want to say CONGRATULATIONS to the Clare team for winning the All Ireland Hurling Final. We were promised no homework if Clare won, and they did. Being from Clare, it was really exciting. And funny, because my Mom can get quite excited about a match. She went CRAZY. In fact, the whole county did. Buildings were painted in blue and saffron and huge banners were put up. The whole school was decorated with the Clare colours. Somebody even painted an abandoned house yellow and blue in celebration.

Today was also a special day for me, because I challenged my OCD for myself today!

I am so excited. It is only a miniscule thing but it's better than nothing! I was typing on the computer and I hovered over the wrong key with my right hand, which is a big no-no. That has something to do with the idea, "If my right hand was hovering over the key that was wrong, I COULD have used it and messed up the word." That means I was thinking about messing the word up. I liken it to a dangerous individual who, although he has not yet committed a crime, was thinking about it and is therefore guilty.

Of course, I felt that I was going to be punished for 'my hand thinking like that' and usually I would backspace all the way until there was nothing left. I delete and retype my work over and over for almost an hour every time I get something wrong, but that night I was stubborn. I didn't want to lose the work I had made an effort to do for the past half hour. I was a writer, and OCD could put that in its pipe and smoke it.

I came up with a quick excuse to not do the compulsion and carried on writing. My mind was screaming, "What are you DOING?! You idiot, do what you're told!" It picks up on danger that's not really there, but my logical side won out, and somehow I continued to type. My hands got sweaty and I felt a little sick but I did it. My stubbornness shoved the thought away and made it smaller.

I didn't just delay the compulsion. I backspaced it.

I told my parents, and they were really happy and I was too! It was a miniature victory. I performed my daily tasks at a faster rate, so it was a good day.

On a bad day, all I would see would be compulsions. Necessary conversations were treated as unnecessary and irritating interruptions: "Don't come near me to tell me my dinner's ready. Just show me and I'll get it myself. I'm trying to prevent the apocalypse here!"

I was especially bitter to people if they so much as whispered to me during a compulsion. I know it is human nature to have conversations, but I get really frustrated, thinking, "Do you KNOW what you just did to me?! Now I have to restart and you don't even seem to CARE. I don't give a damn whether you like my glasses or whatever at this present moment in time, because I AM TOO BUSY, THANKS TO YOU! ARRGH!"

But then, I got really mad at myself for blaming other people when they were just being kind, and it wouldn't be their fault anyway. I didn't want to be hostile, I just got very upset when my rituals were interrupted.

On a less whiny note, OCD is not something completely alien, and can be understood with a little bit of attention. Many people treat it as a taboo subject, but it doesn't have to be.

Rebecca = Definition of Optimism

Chapter Eleven
Overzealous

30/9/2013

I JUST MADE MY IPOD ASYMMETRICAL! ALL ON MY OWN!

I did it all by myself! It's sitting right there, and I have to write really fast to distract myself. Okay, I straightened it again, but holy crap that felt horrible! To just see it there, sitting in its little crooked position, scared me. I got really nervous, but I had to keep going. I had to. I'm getting better.

Mom says I will always have a touch of OCD and it's something I'll just have to live with. That is okay, because I'm CONFRONTING it. OCD isn't something that can go away. It's embedded in your genes and with you until you die. That may seem grim, but what is worse is ignoring it, and letting it take over. If you are in the middle of OCD right now, you CAN beat it. There will be good days and bad days, but it CAN get better.

Message to everybody: You can do it. You can confront OCD and win. It doesn't even have to be OCD. It could be anything, from shyness to a fear of exams. You'd be surprised by the number of people who get nervous before an exam. My friends are SO scared of doing the Junior Cert.

OCD is a crappy disorder, but it won't necessarily always beat you down, it can also make you stronger once you start to stand your ground with it.

I am skipping happily around the house today. I still do my normal rituals, but I do them faster now and I feel more liberated. I use them, they don't use me.

Today was the best. I'm going to study my head off to improve my grades.

PS: My Mom says I can maybe get a Labrador puppy. I may name it Joey!

✦

Over the course of the next few months, I started to get even better. I was having a great time of it. I was happy with what I had. It was amazing. The compulsions were going by so fast and, the best part was, I felt that I didn't even have to do anything! I thought, "Medication is a misunderstood genius! I love this stuff!" That's not really something a kid should be saying, but I felt wonderful.

I launched myself into new projects. I began to have all these brilliant ideas for books and movies. I was so unapologetically happy. I found myself laughing and conversing with my friends, talking at great speed, and it felt so great when they laughed.

They liked me! I wasn't the weirdo who won't say words anymore, I was a comedienne!

I was convinced I could do anything. I was realistic, but extremely optimistic at the same time. I was so happy, I finally felt like I didn't need OCD.

I was even able to tackle my fear of wood knots.

So, that's what I did. I could do it because I was awesome.

I was sitting on Mairéad's hairy chair, inwardly exploding with power, but on the outside all you could see was an extremely agitated kid, hopping her leg, laughing out loud, rubbing her hands and talking way too fast. She peered at me.

"How has your appetite been?"

I replied, "Hungry", which made my parents laugh.

When everybody laughed, I felt great. I felt like the most charismatic person in the world. I wouldn't have felt better if I were on a stage, making whole crowds laugh. I was extremely happy.

"So what have you been up to?"

This was my cue. My cue to talk at rapid speed about everything I did since the last time we met, while hopping my leg up and down. I talked about my projects. I talked about everything. I made many jokes. I was really happy and charismatic. I was talking so fast, I could be an auctioneer.

My doctor turned to my parents, "Is she like this a lot?"

They nodded. "Yes. Most of the time.". They had noticed I was a little hyper. I thought nothing had changed. I was just really happy.

"Just make sure she doesn't get a little too ... high on this medication," Mairéad said. I looked at Mom. High? You can't get high with medication like this! Or so I thought.

At the time, I thought he was making just a general statement. I didn't think it applied to me. I was invincible, after all. I was too happy.

Happy. Happy all the time. So happy that I wouldn't get to sleep at night. I'd be laughing at the most trivial things and thinking I was the best. I didn't miss the sleep either. I had too many projects to think about and, whenever I tried to write them down, my hand wouldn't move fast enough, so I quickly got even more hyper and began to hop my leg or rub my hands.

"So, are we ready to tackle the wood knots?" she said. I would quickly get over the wood knots. It would be trying at first, but I had so much confidence, I would find it easy!

So, we decided we'd tackle them. I was ready for it. When we got home, I told Mom that I was ready for it, and I could see she believed me.

"It's easy, Rebecca, just look at them and not do a ritual. Imagine how free you'll feel."

I would feel free. It would be great to be rid of this compulsion. I would actually be able to go around my house with my eyes open for the first time I can remember.

So, I just looked at a wood knot and turned away from it. I was about to plug in my computer, when I saw another one out of the corner of my eye. Another wood knot.

"Crap!"

Immediately this urge built up inside me to atone for my 'crime'. Simply looking at the wood knot felt like a huge mistake. It felt like a crime to me. Not just a simple action. A crime. I was a murderer. The build-up of anxiety was immense and so sudden. It was like a wave crashing over me, and the guilt came surfing in with it. I felt like I was drowning my best friend.

Because in a way, that is what I was doing.

While I was trying to kill my friend, I decided to go online and look at videos to pass the time. The huge black hole of time dragged as slowly as a wet week. The bright colours of the video and the stupid comments took my attention, but the wood knot was always at the back of my mind. It was waiting for me to pay for my crime.

That sounds crazy doesn't it? But with my OCD, everything has a life. Everything waited with conviction to jump out and accuse me like a prosecutor. But, equally, lawyers can be present too, to work on behalf of the accused, if they can be listened to. It can become a Court of Justice. The possibility of liberty is weighed on the evidence given.

My evidence is logical. OCD's isn't.

I think I'm going to win this one.

The next time I checked, I was about three minutes into the video and suddenly I became aware of what I was doing. I forgot about the wood knot. I forgot about the little dot in my peripheral vision.

It wasn't a literal blackout, where you go from one side of consciousness to the other without any recollection about what happened in between. You are painfully aware the whole time. I saw that dot all through the videos. It was there, poking me.

Have you ever had music stuck in your head? Now, picture your least favourite, annoying song, the one that makes you want to scream if kept on repeat. That's what OCD is like, except the music is replaced by images of your family dying in a bloody massacre. And it keeps playing.

They say that singing the birthday song will get rid of it. I tried watching videos to drown out OCD urges, and it seemed to work. The wood knot guilt trip was gone in a matter of minutes. Placebo? Possibly. Effective? Definitely.

Simple. No more interference. I can now do what I want to do.

Then the wood knot knocks again. Distraction time! It worked before, didn't it?

As the video kept playing, my friend tugged at my sleeve, trying to get me to play with him, like an annoying pest of a little sister or brother, bugging you. Older siblings tell younger ones to go away, or else.

For a moment, I contemplated taking him up on his request to play, just to get him out of my hair for a while, but I soon became the angry older sibling. I didn't WANT to play with him. Why should I? I wanted alone time. Time for myself.

So I told my friend to go away, or else!

He didn't like it. He became angry and abusive, screaming words he shouldn't know at the age he doesn't have.

"What are you doing, you idiot?! Do as you're told! You make me sick!

Everybody will contract a disease because of your stupidity!"

I can't pretend I fully ignored him. It was terrifying, saying no to OCD, yet there I sat, stubbornly refusing. Sometimes you have to be cruel. I then ignored him completely, clicking the mouse in blank areas of the monitor, to underline that my attention was directed elsewhere.

He roared. But quickly it transitioned from a howl of outrage to one of desperation. I was killing him, and he knew it.

He didn't get to play this time.

Then he left. For a while only, but he left. I was left watching my joke video.

"Yo Mama so fat, if she were in Pokémon, her splash attacks would actually do damage."

That's one of my favourites.

Chapter Twelve
Practice

I resolved that the very next time I became triggered by wood knots, I would blatantly refuse to do the compulsions to take away the anxiety. That's easy to say if you imagine yourself taking up that resolution at some vague point in the future, but with OCD, if you make a resolution like that, you could have only a couple of seconds before another trigger hits you, so you'd better be ready.

It was initially a matter of delaying the obsession, allowing the wave of anxiety to wash over me and leave. Because eventually it would. That wave would crash and be gone.

It may feel like it will stay forever, but it honestly doesn't. You have to distract yourself by singing a song or writing. I wrote. I wrote and wrote and wrote. Over a while, I found I had the ability not just to delay it, but also I could completely refuse to do the compulsion. It took a while, but it built up. The confidence built up.

✦

Beating OCD isn't something you do in a day. It is very much a process, a process of constant resistance to internal and external triggers over the course of a long time, in the face of many conditions.

One of the aspects that makes it so hard to deal with, is that it preys on your moods, specifically bad moods. Sometimes, I would come home from school grumpy, just because I am a normal, moody teen. Those were the days I most wanted to give into the obsessions and tap my nose until it hurt. It was stressful having to keep up the process of resistance, but I stuck with it. You need both a lot of patience and impatience. It takes time but, if you're willing to try, you'll get there.

After about two weeks of resistance, my wood knot compulsion had lessened, and by week four, the compulsion was gone. I never did it again.

Everything was becoming easier.

Projects were piling up. I wrote incessantly and made movies. I never finished any of them.

The most ridiculous ideas for movies I saw as being the most inspirational stories I could ever tell. I whipped out the camera at the drop of a hat, and filmed myself talking, feeding the dog, and just generally being funny in my eyes. Because, when I was happy like this, I was convinced I could do anything. Maybe that's the kind of mindset you should have anyway, but I took it to extremes. I was kicking OCD's butt, and I didn't regret it, because I had all these projects to take its place. I would spend the night tossing and turning and coming up with all these new ideas. I would pretend to interview myself on TV and tell everybody about my latest masterpiece.

I started writing this book. I would sit in the kitchen for hours, writing it all down.

At school, I found myself telling ridiculous jokes. I was described as hyper, which was brilliant. During lunchtimes, I would get my habits done quickly, and continue to be everybody's entertainment (in my eyes, at least), and I was perfectly happy with that.

It was great to be funny. It was great to be everything but anxious. It was luxurious.

I felt like that until the next doctor's appointment. I was just as hyper as before, and excited about everything. I couldn't sit still and my thoughts kept racing. I would talk so fast, jumping from one topic from another, that it was hard to keep up.

Dr McGovern was pleased with how I'd beaten the wood knots, but told my parents it was time to reduce medication, before I got 'too high'. Of all the reactions I could have had, I blurted out, "What's so bad about that?"

My Mom just stared at me, like I'd said 'parsnips' (my Mom loathes parsnips). She turned to look at my doctor who explained, "Sometimes, when you get too high, it's hard to get back down. You'd need a hospital. Major tranquilisers."

"You'd be sick", Mom interjected.

I thought tranquilisers were darts from those big guns used on elephants. I pictured myself being shot with one of those and grabbed harder onto the couch.

"It's not fair. I won't be as happy if you reduce the dose. I'm having a great time. I'm fine", I said, speaking in bursts of indignance. I was angry because I thought it wasn't fair. This was the happiest I had been in ages. Surely they weren't trying to make me sad, were they?

"You'll be just as happy with less medication as you are now. You'll be fine," the doctor said.

"Damn it." I clutched the couch.

"Anyway, what is the next compulsion you're going to tackle?"

"The colour one. I'm doing that next."

The doctor looked to my Mom for an expression of confirmation, which she quickly gave. She turned to me.

"Remember how you'll do it?"

I nodded. "See a trigger, don't do a compulsion."

She laughed. "You could try distracting yourself by singing a song, or talking to your friends. You could write it down".

"I do. And I just say no. It works."

It did work. And it still does. When we went to the pharmacy to get my adjusted meds, I saw the blue floor that matched the medical centre's one perfectly. The communal hygienic linoleum that makes the place look like a hospital stretched out across the floor in front of me. And boy, did I see it!

Just like with the wood knots, my Mom didn't take my hand and tell me not to worry, that we'd be out of here soon and that I wouldn't have to see it. She walked to the counter with me following behind. She gave me a pat on the back and proceeded to talk to the cashier. We had agreed on complete BLUE OCD assassination when we had left the doctor's office, effective immediately.

It felt extremely scary gulping in air while looking at the colour, but I quickly felt hope springing up. While trying to kick the the wood knots, I had felt anxious for a long while after the meeting with the doctor. With blue, as a result of my previous success, I was already beginning to feel better, and we hadn't even reached the car park!

I had forgotten what it was like to be 'out of my own way'. I needed to escape my own mind, and my friends helped immensely with that.

With my friend Sylvia now in the school, I met her cousin and his mates. My other friends knew them too, and there was just a brilliant sense of community between us. There was a wider group of friends than I'd had in First Year. Whether it was eating, or arguing about which horror film character is best, there was always something happening. I loved the fact I could look across the hallway and recognise the back of somebody's head. I loved that I could say hi to people that I knew. My friends and acquaintances are the best people in the world.

Second Year was turning out to be great. I began to do well in my tests. It was a great thing to get a mark of over 50%. For my parents, that made their day. Other people were surprised when I told them I aimed that low for my grades, but my 55% was their 99%. People thought it was mediocre, but this was just the beginning. Soon I would get 99% for real.

The reduction in medication in November didn't seem to have a significant effect, yet, over the next few weeks, I started to move less hyper-ly. My thoughts calmed and returned to a 'normal' rate.

I didn't have as many ideas for projects and this made me angry with Mom. I thought it was a mad idea to reduce meds when I had been getting so creative. Surely she could see that the only way I could be successful was to keep a happy attitude. Mom disagreed, saying creative ideas come at a high cost if you get them while you're high.

I dumped another compulsion in November: the Doorway Ritual. I was just having a really good day. Without the wood knots or blue to stop me, I was really up for anything. It's like I had discovered a new superpower.

I had forgotten what it was like to run around my own house as I had spent so much time being scared of it and its multitude of triggers. I got tired of dreading every doorway so, with encouragement from my parents, I started to hop straight through them without a backward glance. I was euphoric.

I stopped acting quite so crazy in front of my friends (although they may deny that) and making quite so many jokes. Everything was okay. That was good, because Christmas was coming!

My parents promised that 2013's Christmas would be a special one. That I wouldn't have to do anything I didn't want to do, unless they asked me to (even then, I'd haggle a little).

On Christmas Day, we would all be getting together to have a big meal in the special dining room at Nana and Grandad's house. I woke up early that morning and raced into my parent's room, because I could. I jumped on the bed and straightened the clock on the bedside table before shaking them awake. We ran downstairs through the hallway to our presents. Mom was so excited she yanked open the front door, threw both arms upwards and screamed, "MERRY CHRISTMAS COUNTY CLARE!" That was followed by an awkward, "Oh, hi!" as she noticed my Grandad was standing in the middle of the field next door. Dad and I fell about laughing. My cousin came and stayed over for a couple of days and I spent the rest of the time eating leftover turkey and ham sandwiches. I got some awesome presents. I got two big box-lights for filmmaking and a new camera. I also got some Japanese stationery (I LOVE stationery!).

I will use anything to my advantage – always. With or without OCD.

Cleaning out the playroom a few days ago, I found a Christmas request I had written in the throes of OCD. When listing what gifts I'd like, I decided to write down the most outrageous things I could think of: an iPhone, a new computer, a TV, a Nintendo XL 3DS, a new camera, you name it. I put a little waiver at the bottom that said, "You may think these requests are a little spoiled and ambitious, but since I'm your lovely daughter who's fiercely battling her killer OCD, I think I deserve it."

I milked it for all I was worth. It's not sneaky, it's efficient.

Baby steps that seemed insignificant at the time, resulted in recovery for my family and myself. Six months previously, it would have seemed impossible to arrive at the point where I could actually see myself getting better. It was brilliant to see what we could actually do. The only things I was still wary of were crooked things and bad numbers/words.

Over the next few months, I began to chase away more compulsions with the courage I got from discarding the old ones. I signed myself up for a local theatre school without telling my parents. They were shocked and amused the next day to receive a call from the theatre school's Principal, who told them I had submitted all the right information online ... except for the credit card number.

I continued to improve at school, and became interested in many more activities. I stopped myself from avoiding cracks and ran around the school area for the first time in a year. I became giddy with happiness, like I had been given a thousand Euro to spend.

I saw new possibilities, now that I didn't have to avoid cracks. I could run and jump and do whatever I wanted. It was brilliant. This meant I could actually keep up with my school friends as they walked around.

I also managed to stop having to lift my leg higher than everything else in the room and tapping things until they felt right. I could go to my room easily, slip through the doorway and flop into bed. It felt like finding a torrent of million-dollar software on a cheap website. Too good to be true.

But in this case, it was true. As long as I kept myself in check, my OCD would keep disintegrating. And I would keep integrating with my world until the pest was gone for good.

I contacted a local musical society and decided to audition. I didn't get the part I was aiming for, but became part of the chorus, and that was almost as good.

I began to go to the theatre school every Friday. I grew to love it. Initially, I was shocked at how all the kids were so expressive and good at performing. They weren't embarrassed to sing their hearts out to a song, beaming like it was something they truly enjoyed. I was accustomed to the universal rule that if you 'performed' like that at school, you'd get dagger looks.

We had to divide into groups to put a dance together and everybody contributed their ideas. When the kids asked me, they didn't do so to see if I would make a fool of myself, they did it because they wanted to get the task done. I was too shy to do anything much at first but, over the next few weeks, I became more comfortable, and knew we were all working together for a big project – to sing, dance and act the best we could.

It was a little bit hard for me in dance class, because of the counting that went with the routines, "ONE! TWO! THREE! FOUR! FIVE! SIX! SEVEN! EIGHT!" It didn't help me to be a very good dancer. You would see me doing a pirouette (which is peculiar enough), and then stopping mid-spin to tap my nose in fierce concentration.

Another challenge to my 'little friend' was the fact that the theatre school building was in the shape of a decagon. That meant there were ten sides, with each room being a crooked segment inside. This made it extremely hard to straighten anything. How do I know if anything is straight if I'm lining it up with the surroundings, and the entire surroundings are crooked?

In the words of the woman on the YouTube viral video, "Ain't nobody got time for that."

Because of all my new activities, I had no time for rituals, so I began to cut down more and more on the ones that were left. I became so cheeky, I challenged my parents to stop smoking completely and see if they could do it at the rate of my ERP, and that, if they couldn't, I would get a present of my choice. Unsurprisingly, they didn't agree to this, and so I began to tease them, saying, "You're still smoking cigarettes while I'm almost rid of OCD! You poor souls, you want to stop, but you can't! Would you like me to help?" It was very light-hearted. They laughed, saying eventually they would give up. I knew they wouldn't, but Mom did cut down – a bit.

In school, I listened in class, put my hand up and began connecting informative dots based on what I learned. My friend Sylvia knew about my OCD better than any of my friends, and we joked about it a lot too.

My parents were thrilled that I could joke about the events of last year. Even now, I draw a crooked line inside their birthday cards to make it a little amusing. It's like our trademark, as much as signing my name on the back of every home-made card, except this one is a little funnier.

✦

The visits to my doctor were becoming less frequent. This was because I simply didn't need to go as often as I used to. I didn't go to my therapist so frequently either, and I was fine with that. I was too busy anyway.

However, I had to keep going, however rarely, because my OCD still had a slight grip on me and my grades.

I needed to take on another compulsion. I knew I had a selection to choose from. I could stop avoiding bad words, I could stop avoiding bad numbers, or I could stop straightening things. Mom thought it would be best for schoolwork that I stop avoiding bad numbers and eventually the bad words would follow. I agreed with that, although it certainly was easier to decide that when you were at home with the comfort of the TV and not standing outside a doctor's office ready to go cold turkey. But I'd been down this road before and I knew where all the roadworks and potholes were, and how to deal with them.

I knew if I slipped in my practices of refusing a compulsion, it wasn't the end of the world. If I do a compulsion even though I'm supposed to be resisting them, I know it's okay, as long as I keep trying. As long as I was trying, my parents were happy. They were, but I wasn't. I wanted OCD out of my life. I'd had enough, and decided if I couldn't go cold turkey, I wouldn't do it at all.

So, on a February day in the doctor's office, I started to resist the 4 Compulsion. I was nervous as we left the medical centre, because it meant that the 'talking' had finished. I'd have liked to talk to the doctor all day if it meant I could put off resisting 4. Even so, I saw that I had to do it. I now believed in CBT, ERP and in myself.

Don't get me wrong, I wasn't completely confident. I liken it to sauntering into a hospital to get an injection, expecting no fear at all. Some people may not mind injections, but, for the majority of people, an injection is an event which, although it does not harm you, will cause some discomfort and apprehension. OCD resistance is like that. There's always that fear. But you have to take it on.

So, when Mom and I were on our way back to our house and she tentatively asked, "Rebecca, what time is it?" I made her wait until I could announce that it was 4:44pm, so I could really knock it out of the park.

She became the happiest person in the whole world to know the time. She started clapping her hands and high-fived me, while swerving (with the one hand she didn't have around my shoulder) to avoid a huge lorry.

After the brief period of swerving and swearing, she continued to freak out, in a happy way, saying, "Well done!" over and over again. I accepted this gratefully, while another part of me was mentally chewing my nails, still dreading what might lie ahead. 4 meant death to me, so if I said, "Four" I felt there would be an occurrence involving death. That would make me the most selfish person on earth, like I was deliberately causing harm to someone, just so I could do maths.

During these internal arguments, it feels like I'm being pulled between two different worlds. The world where OCD tells me everything I do has outrageous consequences. Then there's OUR world where everything makes much more sense. But, which one should I believe?

Sometimes I got so lost in OCD that I'd believe I was part of a psychic world, and that the only way to keep everybody safe there was to do these compulsions. Everybody on Earth could tell me they were illogical, but I wouldn't listen because I was the 'chosen one' and they didn't have the powers I did. They couldn't see things like I could. They didn't have psychic abilities, and so they could never understand my own, superior logic. They couldn't control people's fates like I could.

OCD will ingrain itself so deep in your mind that it causes you to doubt what's real and what's not. My OCD has been growing all my life, so it's had plenty of time to develop foolproof 'if – then – else' systems for every situation I encounter. The trigger for me used to be changes in routine. That's when I need to get out and talk to people, do something to distract myself. Because if I don't, it'll end up burrowing deeper into my head.

My Mom understands this, and continued to drive the journey home, pointing out various landmarks as we drove through the local village. She meant to distract me from the imminent anxiety and it worked. It continued to work until its purpose was lost and I had calmed. I stopped dwelling on an alternate universe where I could control everything. I stopped the voice in my head from pestering me and I locked it out of this world.

We arrived home and I shouted "FOUR!" at my Dad, who had a similar joyful reaction to Mom's, minus the swerving and swearing, as he was not driving. My parents were so thrilled, it almost looked like they had won the lottery. 4 was still an ongoing project, but I was very happy with the progress I had already made.

Similar encouragement was given in my Maths class during the following days, where I was writing the number 4 for the first time this year. My teacher noticed my writing of the dreaded number, and said, "Well done". I was extremely happy. It was exciting getting recognition. That seemed as crazy as writing the number itself.

I took this opportunity to try a bit harder in maths, now that I knew there wasn't an inevitable numbers blockade throughout my efforts. I looked to the other kids around me and asked the teacher what we were doing, and what page we were reading. I wrote a bunch of nonsensical numbers and letters down on the page (with fours!) and after explanation from my teachers and classmates, it became clear which part of the course we were covering. That was promising to me. I knew I could build on that if I tried. So I did.

Now, I understood what the teacher was saying and for once, could dare to put up my hand to ask a relevant question. I wouldn't have asked a question previously, unless as a distraction to escape the scenario where dreaded numbers were being discussed. This time I asked a question *because* of the numbers. And, what's more, I understood what I was asking and what the answer was and how it fitted into the enquiry I had made. I could participate in Business class and Maths class now, so that was a big plus. I could write all multiples of 4.

It affected other subjects and even conversations. I could say the name or number of anything I wanted. It wasn't just a single ability I had gained. I became more confident in general. OCD isn't just a habit. It makes you hate yourself.

I started becoming assured around my friends now that another particle of OCD had dissolved. The anxiety was still there every time I said 4, but I willed myself to keep saying it until it lessened. And it did. This was now my tried and trusted method.

And, soon after that, because I could now say 4, I could now begin to say words like 'death, cancer, dying, morgue, dead, funeral', and others. It was like reading a dictionary to expand your vocabulary. I now had more things to talk about. I frequently use the topic of 'death' or similar 'scary' things in my art projects. It's not because I want practice saying the words I don't like, it's because those topics make for an interesting art project. In fact, my art teacher now expects it of me.

Art class has also helped a lot in defeating OCD. My friend Caitlin sits beside me in class, and we do our drawings together. Also, we just mess around. Whatever it is we do in class, we always do something ridiculous and funny to liven it up. She knows about my OCD and so, one day when

I was straightening markers on the worktop, she reached her hand out and pushed them, splaying pens everywhere. My careful, colour-coded, straight symmetrical arrangement was ruined. I couldn't get mad though, so I converted the anxiety into laughter. I cursed at her and crawled under the table to pick the markers up. I began to laugh and shoved her. She shoved me back and we were both splitting our sides laughing. She laughed even more when I began to straighten the markers again to get them perfect. I couldn't help it, I found it funny too. Her action wasn't malicious, just playful.

If that wasn't enough, my art teacher decided to come over at that exact moment. "What are you girls doing?" she asked as she saw me straightening the markers. I opened my mouth and told her in between guffaws that my markers had been compromised.

"Well, good," my teacher said, "because I know you'll beat that thing." And with that, she reached out and knocked the newly-straightened markers all over the table again. We both looked at our teacher in shock and burst out laughing. My face was red as I straightened them again, but I was laughing equally as hard.

Laughing at myself and OCD! It seemed so small when shared with people. Maybe the isolated world of personalised anxiety I had been living in wasn't as exclusive to me as I thought it was. Friends and teachers seemed to understand and make fun of it in a way that separated me from the OCD. To them, that may seem routine, but for me, it was miraculous. This experience made me see OCD was an acceptable thing to admit to, that you could laugh about it.

If my friend said the room was untidy, I told her I'd come to the rescue. I was great at cleaning up after art projects. I'd always make jokes about being tidy, knowing I could use it to my advantage. The teachers laugh when I make those kinds of jokes. They understand, and my friends do too.

From that day on, I continued to fight to the death, the cancer, the hospital, the morgue, the funeral and the 4.

I wasn't going to give up until I had beaten it.

Chapter Thirteen
Lately

"So, Rebecca, where are your parents going out to tonight?"

I am sitting in the front seat of a car with my aunt, in the dark, pizza boxes staining my lap with steam. My parents have gone on a night out with friends. I am staying at my cousin's house again. I always stay at my cousin's house when my parents go out. I have done it so many times I forget to get worried.

We have picked up a close friend called Rob from the local bar and are going to drop him to his house before returning to our own. Upon collection, my Aunt informed me, "He's a bit sozzled."

That was the first shock. Not that my relative's friend was drunk, but that I started laughing. I laughed because people are funny when they are drunk. They are happy and merry. I knew Rob was drunk from the minute he got in. His ringing chorus of, "Who's in the front seat?!" and upon explanation, "Heeyyyyyy Beckyyyy!"

My Aunt rolled her eyes at me and resumed driving.

The chat continued as we drove through the dark town with the bright yellow sulphur lamps giving that 'night time town' feeling. Rob began asking questions.

"So, Becky, your parents are going out?"

"Yes."

"Where are they going?"

"I know they're going to a bar in town."

"Yes, but which bar?"

"I don't really know."

"How can you let them do that? What if your parents got in a crash or a disaster happened and we'd have to go looking for them? What if they were in danger? Did you ever think of that?"

And with a shock, sitting in the flowing darkness in the front seat with a pizza box and a steamed-wet lap, I realised I hadn't. I never gave a second thought to the safety of my parents. I never thought of my usual escape plan if the impossible happened. But I was not panicked or guilty. I was euphoric.

This was a huge step for me. This meant I could think of other things while being away from my parents, without fixating on their safety. The worst effects of OCD were long gone, and now the anxiety was beginning to trail away too.

In that moment, I felt at ease, sitting in the front seat and laughing politely, like a normal person. Rob now personified my usual anxiety and, for the first time, I got to see how ridiculous it was.

I never had a problem standing up for myself when it came to conflicts with other people. I was sure of myself and what I knew and, pretentious as it sounds, I knew I was always right. Humans are supposed to believe their brains. They do everything by them. I am sitting here typing this thanks to a bunch of connections in my brain I don't even understand. But when an illness takes over, you aren't so sure of yourself because it affects your judgement.

Seeing anxiety personified as someone fretting for nothing, like Rob was, made it so much easier to rise above it and fight.

OCD and anxiety would be so much easier to fight and defeat if it was in the form of a physical person, an external being, so I could see what I was up against. But it's not. It's inside our brains, our most intimate and intricate judgement centre where nothing is supposed to go wrong. But sometimes it does, and when that happens, we can't see past it. And, when it does, affected people try to shove it under the carpet.

I've taken another step.

Caitlin hit her head on the underside of the workbench again. To somebody who is not hyper, it's not that complicated to retrieve a dropped eraser. But we were hyper, and were laughing at so many different things, that even bumping your head off the workbench could be funny. Especially now that it was almost a tradition during Third Year art class.

We collapsed again, hitting the table in a silent, torturous wheeze of laughter. You know the kind. Where your face is frozen into a screaming shape and you bend lower and lower with your stomach muscles begging for you to stop. But you can't, because that'll just start you off again. Your face turns red and your eyes are squirting so many tears of laughter you can barely see the disapproving glance of the teacher.

That happens a lot now.

Sometimes my teacher tells us off because we talk so much and laugh so hard. Our large art room is so thinly populated that we can sit at one end and laugh at the funniest things while doing projects, and people don't hear us. At least, that's what we like to think.

My art project is coming along well now. I originally went with basing it on a line from one of my favourite songs, 'Northern Downpour', but I wasn't happy with how it came out, so I started afresh, this time using something from one of my favourite horror films as inspiration. This project is for our Junior Certificate, which is supposedly 'extremely important'. The difference in workload from Second Year to Third is tremendous. Some people think it is, some people don't, but if I want to get a good job in the future, I should probably work hard now.

Study has always been a challenge for me, not just because of OCD. There are so many things you could be doing. Like talking to your friends, eating a sandwich, playing Minecraft or singing. I sing a lot now. I sing when I do my homework. I sing when I get wood for the fire, and I sing in various choirs in my school, stage school and musical club. Some people tell me I've got a good voice, and that is really exciting. I didn't know I could sing!

There's a lot of stuff to do. I like to write down ideas for films and books when I can. I hate being bored. I think everybody does.

It's hard to sit still in front of schoolbooks when you just want to get up and move around. I want to play on a games console. I want to watch Judge Judy tear the face off some old lady on TV who wants a wedding ring back from her deadbeat ex-husband. It's like everything around me is a toy I can pick up and examine. To be honest, it feels really strange to be able to do the things I like to do.

A while ago, I had to print out the face of the girl from the Exorcist movie for another art project so I decided to do it in computer class. I saved the image, installed the printer and prepared to print. Except, the printer and fax machine names were very similar and I may or may not have sent three copies of Regan McNeil's face to the Head's office by accident. I don't think they'd expect to get a fax like that. If only I was there to watch their reactions!

We're holding a Christmas concert at school soon, which also means it is nearly my birthday. In fact, it is in two days! I will be fifteen and even bolder than before! I wonder what my presents will be. For the concert, I am singing two lines of a Christmas song and I'm also playing the role of Angel Two. It's a very sassy character, but I think I'd be more suited to play the devil, if I'm quite honest with you.

The school choir has also started up again, and it's run by the chaplain that helped me in Second Year. I auditioned, and managed to get a solo in one of the Christmas carols. There is so much to do, and I must say, I love this time of year at school! I also like it at home. We only have three days until we break for Christmas, and I'm excited. Knowing the teachers, we will probably be getting a million pages of work to do over the break. We are Third Year students, after all.

Sometimes you need to keep yourself busy. You need to get involved with everything that school has to offer, and more besides. The problem is, nobody knows what they need until they need it. And by then it's often too late, and too far gone to do anything about it, at least for a while.

Sometimes people with OCD become attached to their obsessions and compulsions because other aspects of the world are not enough. We aren't spoiled, we're idle. We need work. We need engagement, and if we don't get it, we spend too much time in our heads.

It can be perceived that a person who spends time 'inside their head' is automatically deemed to be smart. It is very smart to analyse the world inside your head instead of blurting out everything, as I sometimes do. But then again, if people spend too much time inside their own heads, it can wreak havoc.

So, get out of your head. Study, but also get involved in activities in your area. I sound like a teacher, or a counsellor, but maybe they're saying these things for a reason. Anybody can say, and mean, those words, but maybe it sounds better coming from a kid who's been through it. Sadly, it's only ever adults who say those words, because us kids are all built on an instinctive system of appeasing each other's neuroses to look 'cool.'

Even when my OCD was making my life hell, I went to an art camp, a stage school, two productions and two shows. My friends took me places. I began to write what you are reading. This book kept me from exploding. I had to keep myself busy all the time. Because my mind keeps going and going and if it doesn't have something to latch onto, it just implodes and grabs at obsessions. OCD is an idiot, but I can see the method in its madness.

As my Dad recently said, there is much more to a person than their illness. Illnesses such as OCD are not a person's whole personality. Behind every case of OCD is a regular person with their own traits and talents. OCD is just your classic high-school bully. A separate source of deprecation. A kid that gets badly bullied loses confidence, belief in himself and ultimately, his happiness. But, that kid is still the same. He still has his own character and essence, like everyone has.

People with OCD are often thought to be intelligent people. It takes a lot of brain power to worry every day. It shows your brain is overworking, because whatever is happening in your life at the moment may not be stimulating enough. That's why we're always told to keep ourselves busy.

The level of worry an OCD brain is capable of is equivalent to the level of awesome things that same person is capable of. That dedication could be put into something constructive. It could. But an OCD-affected brain won't let you do it.

We are capable of amazing things and, once we get rid of the little bully, we can do whatever we want.

People with OCD are thought to be detail-oriented, but they can also be artistic. That could be why we have such specific and rigid compulsions. Sometimes I need to get involved in projects and obsessions so much because, if I didn't, I'd go crazy.

Everybody with OCD is absolutely amazing and nobody should doubt that for a second.

It can be very scary, wondering whether you can ever stop the relentless need for control. Sometimes I wonder if I'll ever be free from worry. But this is not likely. If I were free from worry, there would be something wrong. Although my OCD has left me, I still get obsessive thoughts as much as once every two weeks or so. That may be due to a reduction of medication, or perhaps it's just the way I think.

Part of me is a worrier and always will be, but that's also the part of me makes me creative and detail-oriented and I'm happy being like that. I now get ideas for my movie-making all the time – from out of nowhere.

It's amazing to be able to get spontaneous GOOD thoughts.

It's hard to be definitive with OCD. I'd like to be able to say it will never come back and I'll never have another worry in the world, but I can't. On multiple occasions, OCD has tried to push its way back. At any time, I could get a thought that went, "If you don't push your chair up to the table, your father will die". Or, "Your parents will go on a night out and get run over by a car because they're having too much fun and not looking where they are going." Sometimes, thoughts like these come in urges and, automatically, I almost obey them. But I know, if I do that, I may become dependent on them again, so I continually keep an eye out for little thoughts that make me feel scared.

You have to be incredibly mindful when you get the sporadic leftover obsessive thoughts. I can almost picture a little creature scratching at the wooden door in my head, trying to make a hole to get back in.

I've used many analogies for OCD, but my favourite is the little creature. It's little because it's powerless. It's like those kids at school that always want your attention and go to such lengths to get you to acknowledge them. I will never acknowledge OCD, no matter how hard it tries, but neither will I forget about what it can do.

My Mom still regularly checks my hair for patches where I may have pulled it out, even though I haven't done that since 2013. She stills messes up items in my room and regularly checks in with me to see if I had any 'thoughts'. This is a long way from what life was like three years ago, when it would take me two hours to get upstairs and another hour in the morning to get back down. When I did my homework for my teachers, not for me. When I couldn't talk to people and had to leave the house through a window. When I couldn't even get to the window. When I hid in the bathrooms at school and bit my arm because I was so angry and scared. When everything I said was watched by Big Brother, OCD, who would bombard me with horrible thoughts if I said anything definite, just waiting to punish me for lying. I couldn't tell someone what I did the day before just in case I may be lying.

It turns out it wasn't me that was lying.

I'm glad things have changed. I may have felt that I needed OCD at one time, but, as I began to get involved in more activities outside my own world, the pressure to hold on to it eased, and it became easier to finally believe I didn't need it anymore.

You have many more things than OCD to live for. It will eventually leave you, but not without your help.

Chapter Fourteen
Right Now

What's going on now?

Let's first look back to September 2015, which is when I had finished my Junior Cert and was going into my second last year of school. The Junior Certificate is a huge exam (not as big as the Leaving Cert, which is done in Sixth Year and actually has a bearing on your future), but it's still really important (so the teachers say).

I worked hard for the Junior Cert. I gathered every note I was given from Second Year and got some reprinted from my Irish teacher so I could begin covering what I'd missed. To other kids, it's revising, but, for me, I had never seen this material before. That is why my family and I are extremely organised when it comes to my notes. We laid them all out in different categories on the dining room table so I knew where everything was. I had to learn every verb, irregular and regular, in every tense, and countless chunks of vocab, just like every student. Even so, it was hard to learn two years' worth of work in a couple of months.

I used to dream of being one of those kids who got straight As in their exams and got their name mentioned on the radio. I now realise those kids are the kids who have had their heads in the books since First Year. I am not one of those people, even without OCD. I like to get up and move and jump. Even so, I achieved three As (in Art, Irish and German) seven Bs and a C in my Junior Cert. I screamed when I got the results.

Even though I don't have my Leaving Cert until 2017, we have started preparing. We have already completed the listening comprehensions, which were hard because the speakers on the tape talk WAY too fast.

It's been busy so far this year, so much so that it's hard to find time to study. I've been so involved in my singing (I'm doing a couple of concerts with my school and vocal coach soon!) and socialising, it becomes SO BORING to study. I'm still quite hyper, and that makes it quite a chore to sit down and study, as my mind is everywhere. I now realise I need everything I studied in the past few years to succeed in my Leaving Cert. Only, I didn't learn anything for a large part of those years. Because of OCD, one of the most important years in school has been, for the most part, lost.

The school Principal told us on the day we started Second Year that it was the most important year in the school, where you decide what path you're going to take etc. I'm not going to pretend I really appreciate fully what that means, but I guess I'll find out.

This year, as part of being in Fifth Year, the majority of my Year went on the annual ski trip. My geography teacher of four years, Dr Power brings the Fifth Year groups to different countries every year. A team of five really nice teachers was rounded up and we set off. This year, we went to Trentino in Italy. I was a small bit nervous in the days before we went, but surprisingly, I slept soundly the night before we left. Sure, I was nervous, but I had flown before, and this was a private plane, which felt pretty special. I was so excited to be on an airplane with people from my school. I was so excited to play in snow. I was so excited to experience everything that could be experienced on a ski trip with my school.

And I did.

When I was told that this trip was going to be one I would remember for the rest of my life, I did not dispute it. Being on any overnight trip with my friends was memorable, but to be on an overnight trip with my friends in another country playing in SNOW? I knew it was going to be awesome before it even started.

When we arrived in Italy, I quickly noticed that there was no snow. I looked around me, expecting snow on top of airplanes and Italians sliding around everywhere. But no. No snow. When we got on the bus and headed up into the mountains however, it was a different story. They were snow-capped and the air was cold, even with the heater on. Every kid in our bus pointed towards the window, as if they'd never seen a mountain before. But we really hadn't. At least, not one this spectacular.

When we got to the village of San Martino di Castrozza, where we would be staying, I realised that it was going to be my home for the next week. I stayed in a pretty large room with Caitlin, Hazel and Eva. When we opened the door (after traipsing up five flights of stairs) we all screamed and started pulling at things. Our own hotel room. With the earthly equivalent of Narnia sitting outside.

The first thing Caitlin did was flop on the bed, while I staggered to the window and opened it fully. It was too hot in that room, and I was out of breath after walking up all those stairs. I seemed to have left my common sense back in Ireland though, because I made the decision to leave the window open all night. At about three am, the snow showers tumbled into the room, and I woke at five in a refrigerated meat locker. Well done, me.

For the next six days, we learned how to ski. The boots were heavy and the skis were (necessarily) slippery, but it was absolutely the best sport I have ever 'played'.

The first day I was there, I was homesick and overwhelmed. I get sensory overload a lot, and everything here was different. I wasn't very good at skiing and I kept falling, and was becoming increasingly more frustrated with the fact that I couldn't adapt to the new sport as well as the others. I decided to ring my Mom and talk to her, and burst out crying on the phone, telling her I couldn't do it. Eventually, our phone call finished and I went back outside.

But the teachers helped me realise that I could ski, it just took a little bit of practice. I learned how to do the snow-plough, and how to ski parallel. Once I mastered the green slope, I moved on to a blue-bordering-red slope, and felt extremely professional as I steered by way expertly down the mountain. I was even more professional when I decided to tip Caitlin over into the snow.

One of the coolest parts about the trip were the ski-lifts. There are three types. One, where we are locked into a pod cable-car which pulled us up the mountain, another where we sit on a button ride which drags us up the mountain, and your traditional chair ski-lift, where you pull a bar down and sit on a floating bench. My initial panic at the last variety of ski-lift caused me to drop my actual ski-sticks down into the off-course mountain below. My instructor laughed when he heard that I'd thought I'd have to ski down myself and retrieve them.

The days I spent in Italy were some of the best and most fun days ever. Sometimes, Caitlin and I would run down the street (well, a flat-footed clown walk would be more precise) to the supermarkets and stock up on food. Other times we would go to the souvenir shops, or order pizza from an old man who claimed he knew us (we left quite quickly after that). At night, we hung out in the bedroom or went to a karaoke bar and sang Queen songs. It was honestly amazing. I never thought I could be as independent as I turned out to be. San Martino was a bigger town than I had expected, and there was always something to do.

This was me, a kid, who never in their wildest dreams thought I would be able to be away from home for more than a couple of days, and here I was, almost just as good at doing stuff as the other kids. Eating foreign food (Italian pepperoni pizza is EXTREMELY different to ours) and learning new words are just some of the novelty little things that turned out to be big things when you look back.

I had even been too scared to go on our Second Year trip to Achill Island.

My ski trip is a testament to how a person can grow and gain more confidence, even after experiencing something like OCD. Skiing in Italy was one of the best times I've had.

✦

As you can see, I experienced many things during the course of writing this book, some bad, some wonderfully good. Now that I'm going into Sixth Year, the fact that I will be leaving school quite soon is starting to dawn on me. I will be an adult. A real adult, going to college. But that's okay, because there's so much I want to do, and I want to get started.

I want to go on work experience and meet new people and travel to new places, even if it's just a local town I've never been to before. I want to joke around with the kids in class and make them laugh and play horror games and scream together. I want to continue to playfully insult my friends every day and take part in every musical or concert the county has to offer. I want to make my teachers laugh at some of the seemingly funny things I say. I want to insult my Leaving Cert textbooks in mock anger to my friends, only to turn to them once I realise I need them in order to pass the exam. I want to get enough points in my Leaving Cert to be able to do any course I want. I want to have had so much fun in school that I feel mournful to say goodbye.

Mournful, as in death. Death. Death. Death. 4 times.

＋

If you're a person with OCD, I guess all I wanted to say through this book is, don't give up. OCD is an absolute monster. It will tell you the worst things, repeating the thoughts over and over in your mind until you feel like, quite literally, dying. But never give up. People will tell you to get over it. They will never believe you. When you try to explain it, it comes out as a cheap description of a misunderstood, suspicious person. Your explanations will never do justice to the horrors unfolding in your mind when you're wide awake at 5am and praying to God that you will eventually fall asleep.

The only people who truly know what OCD is like are the people with OCD. And, to those people, please don't give up. You are special and wanted. You can tell others what it is like. You have your own unique talents and, believe it or not, you will be able to see colour again.

There will come a day when you are happy, just because. When you decide to, you'll go into your room and read. When you decide to, you'll draw a picture. When you decide to, you'll take up a new hobby. When you decide to call your friends and go outside for a walk, you will.

For me, the first sign I was starting to see colour again was when I began getting those silent, tortuous bursts of maniacal laughter at the most ridiculous things. That was so cool. Thank you Caitlin, for always providing me with that maniacal laughter.

So yeah, my name is Rebecca Ryan. I am now sixteen and a quarter years old (fun bit of trivia for you there). I live in the countryside with a crazy Labrador (and my parents of course). I go for hot chocolate on Wednesdays and play video games with my friends. I am frequently on the Internet, which is annoying for my parents, as I use up all our data. And here I am, after three years of writing it, not really sure how to finish this book.

It all seems to flow so smoothly for other writers. Should I say something to express closure? That the story has finished? Well, in truth the story is about OCD and that's never over. It's something I'll always have to live with.

I've been lucky enough to be able to document this journey in some detail, and I feel that, whatever happens to this book in your hands, I'll be able to read it myself, as a reminder.

This book is ending, but the story of OCD, and those who live with it, never will. People with any kind of mental disorder show amazing strength every single day. It takes a lot to fight your own mind every day. You guys are and will always be awesome.

The story continues.

resources

OCD Ireland: www.ocdireland.org

OCD UK: www.ocduk.org

Reach Out: ie.reachout.com

Spun Out: spunout.ie

Mentalhealthireland: www.mentalhealthireland.ie

This book's Facebook page: Facebook.com/dictatorshipbook

Instagram: @dictatorshipbook